T0310943

INTERSTITIAL HONG KONG

Exploring the Miniature Open Spaces of High-Density Urbanism

Xiaoxuan Lu   Susanne Trumpf   Ivan Valin

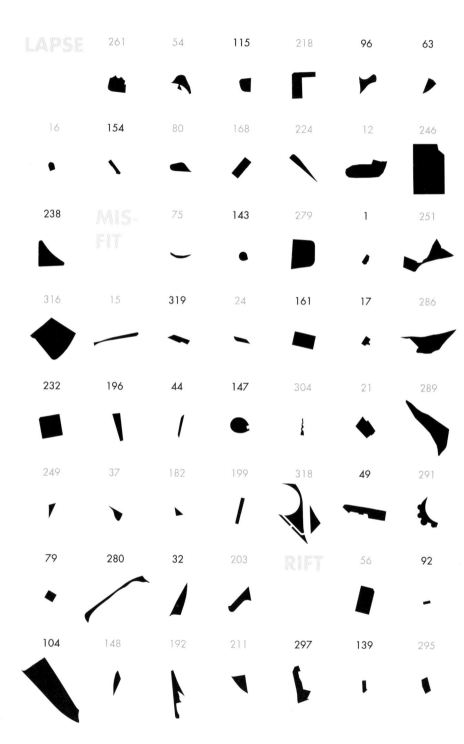

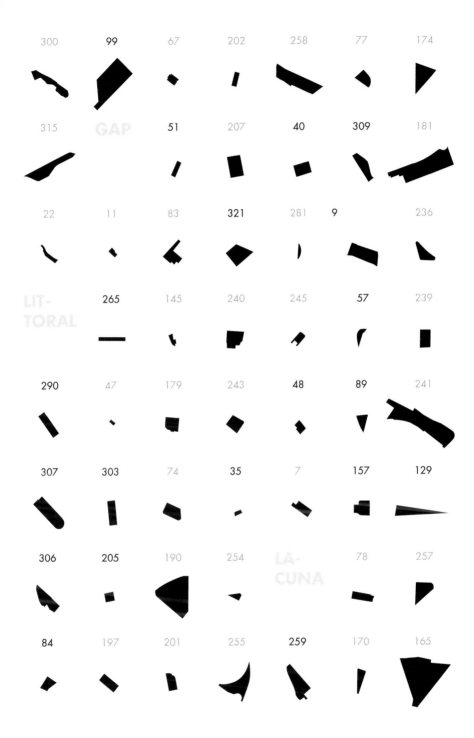

300   99   67   202   258   77   174

315   GAP   51   207   40   309   181

22   11   83   321   281   9   236

LIT-
TORAL   265   145   240   245   57   239

290   47   179   243   48   89   241

307   303   74   35   7   157   129

306   205   190   254   LA-
CUNA   78   257

84   197   201   255   259   170   165

Preface

The research collected in this book originates from our collaborative teaching within a Landscape Architecture master's degree studio at the University of Hong Kong. This introductory studio, which ran from 2016 to 2018, featured a case study exercise aimed at building an understanding of spatial conditions within the finite extent of a small-scale public space. We allocated one Sitting-out Area or Rest Garden case study to each student. Over the course of these three years, and with input from the students, teaching this studio course resulted in the categorization and detailed documentation of 105 sites. In this volume, we look at 42 of these examples, each one a representative of these categories. The initial studies in the studio form the foundation of the research, and the collective work gathered in this book is presented as a catalog of the city's diverse physical and spatial conditions.

Like other books that take a similar methodological approach, such as *Made in Tokyo* (2001), *Made in Shanghai* (2018) and *A Little Bit of Beijing* (2013, 2015 and 2018), our survey attempts to examine a particular urban typology from an impartial perspective, treating each case with an open curiosity and consistent rigor. But unlike those volumes, this exploration of the diversity of small public spaces in Hong Kong is more than a guidebook of typological curiosities; it is an investigation into a city—its processes, its professionals and its people.

The surveys and research work in this volume have been exhibited in various formats in Shanghai, Guangzhou and Hong Kong. Our explorations on the potential of Sitting-out Areas and Rest Gardens within each of our divergent disciplinary interests has opened up a wider discussion among our colleagues and our peers in other disciplines about the role of space, territory, geology, publicness, governance and even pedagogy. We present in this book a new set of individual case studies and widen our scope through a set of original texts in order to reflect on the broader assembly of the high-density city.

PART 2:
Cases

PART 1:
Contexts

Below, between, behind – the Sitting-out Areas and Rest Gardens found in the urbanized areas of Hong Kong Island and Kowloon are invisible at a first glance; they are comprised by amplified densities, hyper-efficiencies, multi-layered grounds and mega-infrastructures.

Introduction

Xiaoxuan Lu, Susanne Trumpf and Ivan Valin

An Ontology of Small Urban Spaces in Hong Kong

Hong Kong has more than 500 Sitting-out Areas and Rest Gardens throughout its urbanized territory. Ranging from 50 to 7,000 sqm, these compact public open spaces are the smallest features of the city's official network of public open-space amenities. Though cumulatively they account for a significant proportion of Hong Kong's open space, Sitting-out Areas and Rest Gardens can be hard to find and difficult to access, and they are generally overshadowed by the city's larger and better-maintained parks. Their ubiquity and uniformity, however, allow them to make a tangible impact, not only on their adjacent communities but also within the larger system of political, economic and environmental relationships. The etymology of the term "Sitting-out Area" is a product of Hong Kong's particular historical context as a British colony. The term can be traced back to late nineteenth-century British English, where it is found in the popular press of that time. The Oxford English Dictionary made "sitting-out area" an official term in 2016, where it appears as a term designating "a place for sitting outdoors" and "specifically (chiefly Hong Kong English) a small public space with seating in a built-up urban area." In Cantonese, the name for these spaces is perhaps the most descriptive: known as *saam kok see hang* (三角屎坑) *or* "three-cornered shit-pit," the term is a tacit recognition of their marginal status among the open spaces in the city.

Parks and greenbelts replicate nature in the city and have long been recognized as providing an essential buffer to the ills of urban life. Nature vs. City is an intuitive and practical dichotomy in the modern, industrializing world that has long formed the backbone of theory and practice in urban and regional planning. But in recent decades, a wide range of disciplines, from hard sciences to post-modern philosophy, have contributed to an expanded notion of nature. Likewise, our understanding of the metropolis has become more nuanced as social scientists and urban theorists have complicated notions of space and publicness in the modern city. The result is a growing discourse on the city *as* an ecology in which urban and natural systems overlap, cooperate and hybridize. Ideas of openness and publicness are far from concrete, but are relative and negotiable. It is in this context that the practice of creating small-scale, opportunistically achieved, networked open spaces has emerged. And it is in this context that Hong Kong's Sitting-out Areas and Rest Gardens must be cast.

Many cities have recently initiated projects to build pocket parks, micro-parks and parklets as a strategy to provide adequate and accessible public open space in densely developed districts. City planners and managers have embraced this new class of green space for its environmental, economic and health benefits. These small spaces, especially when measured together, can be shown to reduce the urban heat island effect and to measurably improve a city's environmental impact through their ecological services. Seen individually, these projects are quick, visible projects – miniature commitments to public welfare at the scale of the street. They have a measurable impact on property values, walkability and social wellbeing. Residents often benefit when small parks can repurpose underutilized or undevelopable sites. But small public open-space interventions can also be tools of urban renewal, diverting public space and investment for private benefit while erasing its pre-existing ecological or social value.

Hong Kong's Sitting-out Areas can be evaluated and critiqued along any one of these dimensions. They can be seen as a legitimate practice of space-making and landscape planning, with the potential to create meaningful benefits for individual sites and for the overall urban system. But unlike the coherently planned and managed micro-park programs in San Francisco, Philadelphia or London, Hong Kong's Sitting-out Areas are the products of an ad-hoc bureaucratic process. Though each Sitting-out Area and Rest Garden contributes to a fulfillment of the city's overall green-space allocation guidelines, there are no clear expectations at the level of the site. This leaves the outcomes related to community, geology, ecology or history, ultimately undefined.

Categories

By collecting and communicating their unifying spatial, material and organizational attributes, our research situates the Sitting-out Area and Rest Garden at the scale of the city and within an urban, social and ecological context. In curating the physical variety and diverse underlying narratives among the surveyed Sitting-out Areas and Rest Gardens, we have created six categories for the individual case studies. The categories frame an understanding of the spatial conditions and the social and environmental values of the Sitting-out Area or Rest Garden and of the underlying challenges of being situated in a city with ever-changing policies. Rather than seeing these as fixed classifications, the six categories should be considered provisional and overlapping – serving to contextualize these fragments of Hong Kong's urban form and creating opportunities for imagining their future potential.

Lapse: Heritage Signifier
At the core of Hong Kong's identity is a story of the transformation of a sparsely inhabited island and peninsula off the coast of southeast China into a global cultural and financial center built to notorious levels of density. Within this evolution, spanning both the colonial and post-colonial eras, there is a constant metabolism of elements from both Chinese and foreign cultures and practices. Traces of this multi-layered and culturally diverse past are visible across the city, giving it a unique and valuable heritage. Some Sitting-out Areas reveal particular details of Hong Kong's history, filling gaps in our collective memory. Other sites contain physical or material evidence of the past, revealing original artifacts or displaying small memorials, signage or design interpretations in deference to the particular heritage value of the site. Some are more tacit in recognizing their heritage, pointing to their histories by celebrating the particularities of the site itself as it transforms from a *place* in the city to an *interstice* in the city.

Misfit: Infrastructural Spanner
Between the 1950s and 1970s, ideas for providing parks were dominated by top-down, large-scale planning approaches that allocated green in a clear hierarchy, from country parks to local central parks. However, with the concurrent rapid expansion of freeway and road networks across this hilly territory, another type of landscape planning emerged to take advantage of the residual spaces that appeared alongside this newly constructed infrastructure. In fact, we find the first references to "Sitting-out Areas" in Hong

Kong in the popular press, such as the *South China Morning Post*, where they were praised as an effective way of transforming roadside spaces into open space for local residents. Today, the city's road and rail infrastructure is multi-layered, robustly engineered and linked to sophisticated property development strategies. Yet the curvatures, setbacks and clearances necessitated by these systems don't fit precisely within the finer-grained urban context, especially in older urban areas, and this results in unclaimed spaces in-between, along or beneath these structures. Sitting-out Areas exploit these leftover spaces, finding purpose in their linearity or taking advantage of their broad concrete coverings.

Rift: Geodynamic Filler
Hong Kong's steep and landslip-prone terrain has always been a challenge to large-scale settlement and infrastructure works. As engineers and geologists began a massive project to reclaim, stabilize or rectify the territory's natural slopes in the 1970s, a new stepped and folded geometry emerged in the city. Today, a network of around 60,000 registered reinforced slopes and even more retaining walls stabilizes Hong Kong's ground. This geometry of functional reinforcement clashes with the geometries of tower-building and transport engineering. The ubiquitous engineered slopes permit real-estate development and roads to climb the slopes of the city, but they also create a profusion of imperfect joints that cannot be captured as capitalized space. These fragments of land, with their miniscule area, are occasionally utilized as sites for Sitting-out Areas. Often invisible from the street, they quietly provide small, non-privatized recreational spaces behind the dense urbanized areas of the city.

Littoral: Terrestrial Anchor
In addition to terracing its steep hills, Hong Kong is also known to expand its developable land area by reclaiming land from the harbor. Much of the occupied city today was once under water. This unnatural waterfront has long been a working edge, too, and is filled with infrastructure for transportation, anchorage, utility in-and-outtakes, flood-protection and erosion control. With economic and social pressures, this water's edge is increasingly being rethought beyond the usual calculations of economy and engineering. Nearly a third of the 161 Sitting-out Areas and Rest Gardens on Hong Kong Island are built on historically reclaimed land. Some of these small public open spaces manage to bring people to the waterfront in new and inventive ways by repurposing outdated infrastructure, revitalizing overlooked gaps in access or adding entirely new layers to the edge. With open views and access to air, water and light, these Sitting-out Areas and Rest Gardens often contain an active

set of programs unlike those found in the city's typical passive open spaces, showing off in these edge sites a recreational, resourceful and environmentally minded Hong Kong.

Gap: Density Deconstructor
Hong Kong's urban metabolism provides additional ground for Sitting-out Areas at a granular level. In the late twentieth century, Sitting-out Areas were used as a tool in urban renewal programs. Informal settlements were once considered a menace to public health and land development, and various interventions were made to restrict the growth of temporary structures on areas that were required for development, or with a view to reducing health, fire or structural hazards. Alongside other practices such as providing fire-breaks, sanitation, drainage works and electricity, Sitting-out Areas served as an effective device to control small pieces of land by marking them out as managed local amenity areas. Today, as planning guidelines and building regulations continue to shift, Sitting-out Areas are activated as small, entirely flexible forms of open space. They occupy the lots of demolished *tong lau* (old tenement buildings) or fill in the irregular setback gaps between large, new complexes. As density targets and lifestyle expectations continually alter the fabric of the city, the Sitting-out Areas absorb the resulting spatial incongruencies.

Lacuna: Ecological Amplifier
Situated within the Indo-Burma Hotspot, one of 25 regions in the world that have contain exceptionally large number of species, Hong Kong is endowed with extraordinary biodiversity. While the relationship between biodiversity conservation and the country parks that make up some 40% of Hong Kong's total area has been well recognized, the bio-ecological functions of the pocket parks dispersed in Hong Kong's densely developed urban areas have only recently gained attention among built-environment scholars. Some of the larger Sitting-out Areas and Rest Gardens showcase a more natural environment and allow relatively abundant planting. These park-like fragments range from islands of designed and managed green space to those with pre-existing vegetation. Given their low importance in the public realm hierarchy, these spaces often lack regular maintenance and are freely colonized by wild plants and weeds, serving as reserves of biodiversity and evidence of Hong Kong's diverse native and naturalized flora.

Chapters

This book offers an analysis of a small but important open-space typology in Hong Kong and an exploration of the potential of Sitting-out Areas and Rest Gardens from different disciplinary perspectives. These different disciplinary viewpoints are unified in their analytical approach to the Sitting-out Areas and Rest Gardens, using a mix of theoretical, empirical and historical motivations – interpreting public open space in relation to Hong Kong's geological setting; drawing attention to the pedestrian network that ties Sitting-out Areas and Rest Gardens to the city and to each other; analyzing the relevance of these spaces in urban planning policies; expanding on adjacencies of other occasionally informal open spaces; and ultimately reflecting on the use of these open space fragments as case studies in the graduate program at the University of Hong Kong.

The opening chapter "Hong Kong *Terra Infirma*" analyzes Hong Kong's ground and examines how the design, construction and upgrading of man-made slopes and retaining structures have shaped the territory's civic spaces. It casts new light on urban socio-natural interactions through a close study of the geotechnical expertise and commitment invested in consolidating the city's historically unstable ground. By bringing into sharp relief the role of geotechnical risk management as a catalyst for institutional change and urban reconfiguration, this chapter challenges the dominant Hong Kong narrative that fetishizes the role of land value and spatial efficiency in the shaping of the city's urban spaces.

The ambiguity of heroic infrastructures and the compromised ground as constituted in the three-dimensional pedestrian network in the city is discussed in the second chapter "Between the In-between." In this text the locations and adjacencies of public open space are interpreted through the overlapping of machine learning, artificial intelligence and human interpretation to assess the current and potential locations of small open spaces in the city. The study analyzes two dense urban areas at a series of scales using a blend of regulatory principles and proposed measures such as frequency, visitation duration, size and accessibility. The findings reflect on the suitability of planned renewal projects and the city's approach to its latest land reclamation and harbor-front renovation projects.

The third chapter "On Imported Planning Policies" examines the history of planning policy in Hong Kong and its role in shaping public open space. Emerging in the context of the rapid urbanization of Hong Kong after World War II, the typology of Sitting-out Areas is positioned as a by-product of attempts to transplant British town planning theory to Hong Kong. Considering the city's dense and ever more built-up context, this chapter argues for a design and maintenance framework that is able to satisfy government requirements and local community aspirations, respond to the unique and contradictory forms and functions of the urban fringe and be sensitive to the ecology of their site-specific flora, fauna and human beneficiaries.

The fourth chapter "Ambiguous Topologies of Public Open Space in Hong Kong" extends the analysis to a larger network of open spaces to highlight the ambiguity of formal classifications. Given Hong Kong's dense, over-built and often vertiginous conditions, spaces have a tendency both to bleed into one another and to be interrupted and disjoined in unexpected and surprising ways. This chapter focuses on the practices that unify many of these spaces, describing the complex connections between spaces and objects. The authors show how localized open space networks help us to understand the ways that people actively occupy, define, create and maintain this system.

The final chapter "Reassembling the Case Study" revisits the pedagogical origins of this research project. Within the context of training the city's landscape architects in a first-semester design studio, the chapter presents an example of a modified case study method, used both to illuminate the unique circumstances of a particular urban condition and to generate reflective design thinking. In studying the everyday nature of Sitting-out Areas, the exercise forces students to deal with the underlying potential of these areas and articulate alternative positions. Challenging the hierarchies of studio education and the typically rigid use of case studies, the chapter argues for an integrated methodology that prioritizes field work, critical thinking and active learning within the outdoor laboratory that is Hong Kong.

Hong Kong's Sitting-out Areas and Rest Gardens have never been considered conceptually, collectively or strategically as a specific typology in the city. This book attempts to weave these abundant small public open spaces into the tapestry of the city itself, connecting their smallness and publicness to the unique forms, textures and narratives that make Hong Kong. In quantity and value, the ad-hoc and accidental Sitting-out Areas and Rest Gardens of Hong Kong already rival the heavily promoted micro-urban space projects in other cities. Yet, within Hong Kong itself, they remain underappreciated as an urban system and undervalued as urban space. Sitting-out Areas and Rest Gardens have yet to realize the true potential of their beneficial impact for the city, its environment and its community. The surveys here highlight these lost potentials while respecting the unique outcomes of each individual case within the city's fabric. Ultimately, these tiny pieces of open space in hyper-dense Hong Kong point to methods for a more deliberate dialogue in this city, one that interweaves small and large; public and private; and green and grey.

Hong Kong *Terra Infirma*:
A City's Defiance of Its Slippery Slopes

Xiaoxuan Lu

A City Without Ground?

Like many, my first glimpse of Hong Kong was from an airplane window as we approached the airport just after sunrise. With the jungle of skyscrapers shrouded in mist and the mountainous terrain disappearing and reappearing amid the rolling clouds, the city resembled a vast magical container ship floating gently into Victoria Harbor.

This first direct impression of the city echoed the intricate "bird's-eye" cutaway views of the multi-layered infrastructure of urban Hong Kong in *Cities Without Ground* – a beautiful and revealing book that had given me my first indirect impression of Hong Kong a few years prior to my personal introduction to its physical reality (Figure 1). Written and drawn by architects Adam Frampton, Jonathan D. Solomon and Clara Wong, the book makes the bold claim that "Hong Kong is a city without ground" (2012, 6). With exploded axonometric diagrams of over 30 key areas, the book focuses on the city's labyrinthine three-dimensional pedestrian circulation networks – the myriad of aerial walkways, elevated bridges and underground tunnels that make it possible to walk around much of the city without ever having to set foot on the ground. The book, which defines ground as "a continuous plane and a stable reference point" from an architectural perspective, portrays Hong Kong as a city that has radically abrogated its relationship with this ground plane, and highlights the resultant horizontal and vertical disorientation one experiences when navigating around the city's tangled web of pedestrian spaces (6).

While its colorful diagrams capture the intricacy of the city's tightly packed circuitry of pedestrian networks, the book simultaneously blinds the reader to the importance of the public realm at ground level by rendering everything outside those architectural structures in a watery light blue. In fact, when looking out of most hotel or office windows, or taking a bus ride through the city, one cannot ignore the mountainous terrain that envelopes the jostling crowds of high-rise buildings. Walking through the elevated or underground pedestrian

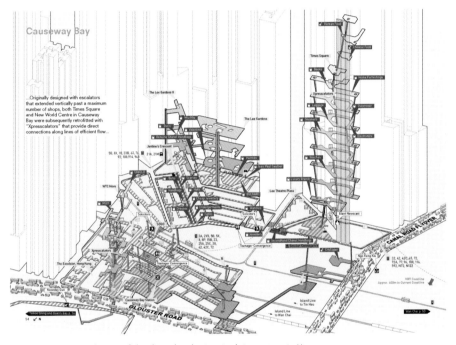

Figure 1. Axonometric diagram of the elevated pedestrian circulation systems in Hong Kong, from *Cities Without Ground: A Hong Kong Guidebook* (2012), by Adam Frampton, Jonathan D. Solomon and Clara Wong

passageways, or the interconnected malls and office lobbies, is an incomplete experience of the city. At some point, the walkway will land you on a street or pop you out onto a hillside path, and you are brought both physically and figuratively back to earth. Whether covered with concrete or vegetation, the steep terrain reveals itself as a landscape carapace or exoskeleton, which although usually viewed piecemeal, contains and coexists with the continuous urban-scaled interior.

The engineered hillsides accommodate a range of civic space assemblages peculiar to their contorted locations. Public facilities and amenities, such as running paths, pocket gardens and bus stations, are often found squeezed between the retaining structures and hairpin bends of the roads that wind their way up the steep slopes. This type of exterior public realm reminds us of the intimate but fraught relationship between the city and its geology. If we look at the "ground" through a landscape architectural or geological eye rather than a purely architectural one, then it can be seen everywhere in Hong Kong. All the stories of this city's construction, whether upwards, downwards or sideways into the sea, begin with the ground, no matter whether it is stable, catastrophically unstable or even yet to be formed.

A City With Ground but no *Terra Firma*

"Ground" and "terra firma" are often used interchangeably. The Latin phrase "terra firma," which means literally "firm land" or "solid earth," encapsulates the feeling of being grounded, in contrast to feeling "all at sea" or "up in the air." The ground is usually associated with safety and stability, but the case of Hong Kong tells a different story. Hong Kong is a city in which the ground is often described as loose and volatile, or in geotechnical engineering terms, "unconsolidated," and where the city's long history of devastating landslides is etched into the collective memory (Bobbette 2016, 525). The inherent instability of its soils and geology, its steep topography, the historical eradication of its original hillside vegetation and its susceptibility to frequent and torrential monsoon rains and typhoons all conspire to render Hong Kong's ground extremely unstable, sometimes to the point of liquefaction.

Since the mid-twentieth century, the accepted narrative of Hong Kong has fetishized how it was land values and spatial efficiency that shaped the city's public and private interior spaces; however, there is another longer and more foundational story lurking literally beneath that accepted narrative. This alternative narrative extols the effort and ingenuity invested in those exterior spaces of the ever-burgeoning city in an attempt to secure it against the forces of erosion that would pull the very ground from beneath it. It is a story that begins with Hong Kong's establishment as a colonial urban center in the mid-nineteenth century, and that continues to this day.

A Decomposing "Barren Rock": Pre–World War II Era

When Hong Kong was ceded to Great Britain under the Treaty of Nanking in 1842, British Foreign Secretary Lord Palmerston famously denounced it as "a barren rock with nary a house upon it." The new colonists frowned upon this newly seized malarial territory, with its steep inhospitable terrain and paucity of flat land, rivers or mineral wealth. Adding to their disdain were the British geologists' findings that much of the ground was unstable. The *Journal of the North China Branch of the Royal Asiatic Society* for 1865 contains one of the earliest published descriptions of Hong Kong's geology, penned by T.W. Kingsmill:

> Before passing on to describe the other rocks, the granites found here will merit our attention for some little time … From the large amount of Mica they contain, as well as from the excess of the Alkaline materials in the felspar forming one of their components, they are readily decomposed, and have yielded to the disintegrating action of the atmosphere (in these regions impregnated with water for a large portion of the year) to an enormous extent, leaving behind a mass of soft, unctuous clay surrounding the grains of unaltered quartz. (1865)

Some three decades later, S.B.J. Skertchly provided a detailed examination of the granite tufts of Hong Kong in *Our Island: A Naturalist's Description of Hong Kong* published in 1893. Referring to Hong Kong as the "Granite City" due to its wealth of granite buildings, walls and stepped streets, as well as the very hillsides that supported them, Skertchly pointed out that much of the granite found in Hong Kong was weak (1893, 11). Feldspar, the small "glassy … white crystals" distributed throughout granite, is dissolved by the carbonic acid in the rain, leaving behind a kind of "unctuous clay." Unlike granites in other parts of the world, which are known for their strength and durability, the granite of Hong Kong decomposes and morphs into a clay that is "a friable mass soft enough to be dug with a spade … to a depth often of sixty feet or more" (13).

Published just before the First Sino-Japanese War (1894–1895), half a century after Hong Kong's establishment as a colony of the Crown, Skertchly's book reflects upon the difficulty in developing the city of Hong Kong under such challenging geological and geographical conditions and reveals an urgent need for further territorial expansion. After the British acquired Hong Kong Island in 1842 and the Kowloon Peninsula in 1860, the colony began to attract large numbers of Chinese and foreign fortune seekers. The population, estimated at 23,817 in 1845, jumped to 160,402 in 1881, and surged to 221,441 in 1891 (Fan 1974, 1). In 1894, an outbreak of bubonic plague forced the Hong Kong Government to confront the appalling overcrowding and rat-infested squalor that prevailed in the older, lower-income parts of the city. The British took advantage of Imperial China's defeat at the hands of the Japanese in the First Sino-Japanese War in 1895 to press for an extension of the colony, leasing the rural New Territories for 99 years under the Second Convention of Peking. This newly acquired land provided for better military defense, as well as additional space for future urban expansion and, in particular, a redistribution of residential areas.

The city dwellers were susceptible not only to infectious diseases due to the lack of sanitation and overcrowding but also to natural disasters. As the population expanded, the number of "boat-people" crammed along the seafronts in unseaworthy fishing vessels and houseboats rose, as did the number of squatters living in rickety shacks perched high on the terraces dug into the steep hillsides. In a climate where typhoons are practically guaranteed every year, and in a terrain highly prone to landslides, catastrophic natural disasters were a forgone conclusion for the rapidly expanding population. One of the earliest records of a landslide causing civilian casualties dates to May 29–30, 1889, when the city was inundated with 33 inches (840 mm) of rain (Geotechnical Engineering Office 2013, 14). On September 18, 1906, Hong Kong was struck by a typhoon resulting in the highest death toll in its history, with more than 15,000 people perishing, countless landslides recorded and nearly 3,000 fishing boats and 670 ocean-going vessels damaged or sunk (21).

The Emergence of a Ground Culture: Post–World War II Era

Between World Wars I and II, landslides were frequent and had tragic consequences,[1] and it was at this time that the government began conducting detailed geological surveys, with a view to taking some precautionary measures and to prepare for post-war development. The first and second versions of the geological report were published in 1939 and 1948 respectively, and 1948 also witnessed the publication of the Hong Kong Preliminary Planning Report by Sir Patrick Abercrombie (known as the Abercrombie Report), which was drawn up for the Hong Kong government to guide the development of the entire territory and contained the first strategic

[1] The two most devastating disasters during this period occurred in the summers of 1925 and 1926. On July 17, 1925, undermined by three continuous days of heavy rains, an extensive retaining wall collapsed and swept away seven houses in Po Hing Fong, killing over 70 people. A year later, another tragic landslide occurred after a total of 534 mm of rainfall on July 19, 1926. Hillside roads were converted into roaring cataracts, bringing tons of rocks, mud and debris down into the urban area. A 3,000-ton boulder hit the Pokfulam Pumping Station, killing workers and cutting off the water supply to the Peak and the Upper Levels.

Figure 2. An aerial photo showing the extent of the deadly landslide at Kotewall Road in 1972, from *When Hillsides Collapse – A Century of Landslides in Hong Kong* (2013), by Hong Kong Civil Engineering and Development Department

plan. Overpopulation and land use conflicts were the most severe challenges encountered by the government during this post-war era.

The population witnessed a dramatic slump during the Japanese occupation (1941–1945), dropping from 1.5 million before the war to an estimated 600,000 in the immediate aftermath as a result of repatriation programs and food shortages.[2] Post-war, the numbers rapidly surpassed their pre-war peak to reach 1.8 million by the end of 1947, bolstered by those who were returning home after the war as well as the floods of migrants fleeing the civil war in China in the late 1940s. The population further expanded to 2.5 million in 1956, exceeding the 3 million mark in 1960, and it had hit almost 4 million by 1970 (Fan 1974, 2).

The amount of developable land in Hong Kong was increased both through reclamations from the sea and through the excavation of terraces into the steep hills on Hong Kong Island, Kowloon and increasingly further afield, to accommodate the rapidly growing population. The accumulation of geological knowledge since the mid-nineteenth century, combined with increasingly intense post-war land engineering efforts resulted in a ground-orientated development culture, or a ground culture, that was first reflected in a series of institutional changes aimed at better responding to specific landslide issues in the 1960s. In 1966, the Public Works Department (PWD), which was responsible for municipal engineering works, land administration and surveys, and building regulations, was assigned responsibility to deal with the complaints related to risks in the squatter areas. Concurrently, the government set up a Landslip and Rainstorm Damage Committee to oversee decision-making on all landslide cases that might constitute damage to persons or property and establishing liability for carrying out remedial works.

The 1970s marked a turning point in Hong Kong's approach to landslides, with dramatic improvements made to the design standards governing earthworks and the related building control procedures, bringing the quality of the unseen foundational aspects of the urban area up to speed with its rapidly developing international façade. This transition was largely in response to a number of disasters that served to highlight the potential severity of landslides, with the population density of post-war Hong Kong having reached unprecedented levels. On June 18, 1972, two fatal landslides, on Po Shan Road and in Sau Mau Ping, took a total of 138 lives (Geotechnical Engineering Office 2013, 77), and four years later, on August 25, 1976, Sau Mau Ping was again in the headlines when four landslides struck the area in a single day killing 18 people and seriously injuring a further 24 (2013,

[2] Due to the shortage of essential resources and the possible counter-attack of the Allies, the Japanese implemented a repatriation policy to force the local Chinese to return to their homes in the mainland.

Figure 3. Slope Registration Plaque: (top) Photograph of a slope registration plate within the University of Hong Kong; (bottom) Civil Engineering and Development Department (CEDD) standard drawing of a slope registration plate

115) (Figure 2). Although there was nothing new about landslides intruding into buildings, overturning cars, destroying infrastructure, and filling streets with mud and boulders in the wet season, the twin landslides of 1972 and the Sau Mau Ping landslides of 1976 were considered especially devastating by the government in the light of its extensive public housing program, which was on the threshold of massive expansion. The fragmented public housing programs that had been implemented since the mid-1950s were replaced by the government's 1973 Ten-Year Housing Program that aimed to provide self-contained accommodation to 1.8 million people between 1973 and 1982 (Town Planning Division 1984, 10).[3]

[3] The ten-year plan was launched to overcome Hong Kong's housing problems and related social unrest, through public housing development, which was aimed at accelerating the development of new towns and their infrastructure and ancillary facilities.

The 1972 and 1976 landslides raised serious questions regarding public safety in the context of these new housing programs, prompting the then governor Sir Murray MacLehose to ask, "Do I have to evacuate several thousand people each time it rains?" (Knill et al. 1999, 4). Hong Kong's unconsolidated ground was beginning to threaten the government's most ambitious efforts to reorganize the territory to date. Soon after the 1976 Sau Mau Ping landslide, MacLehose appointed a panel of international experts to make an independent review of the causes of landslides and to propose measures to prevent similar disasters in the future. According to the Report of the Independent Review Panel on Fill Slopes, the collapsed slopes at Sau Mau Ping were created by "end tipping," with decomposed granite accounting for the majority of the loose fill (Hong Kong 1977, 10). Given that this was common practice for housing development in Hong Kong, the report argued that Sau Mau Ping was not an exceptional case, and that a large and increasing number of slopes throughout Hong Kong were on the verge of collapse. The panel highlighted the need to consolidate the ground prior to any further development, and suggested the establishment of "a control organization" to enforce continuity throughout "the whole process of investigation, design, construction, monitoring and maintenance of slopes in Hong Kong" (41). The Geotechnical Control Office (GCO) of the PWD was formed in 1977 to act on the recommendations of the panel, and since then, the construction and maintenance of properly engineered slopes and retaining structures have become central to all subsequent development in the territory, residential or otherwise (Malone & Ho 1995).[4]

[4] The Geotechnical Control Office was renamed as the Geotechnical Engineering Office (GEO) in 1991.

A City Grounded

The era of landslide hazards, referring to the three decades following the end of World War II, was followed by the era of grounding Hong Kong, after the establishment of the GCO. Today, one can

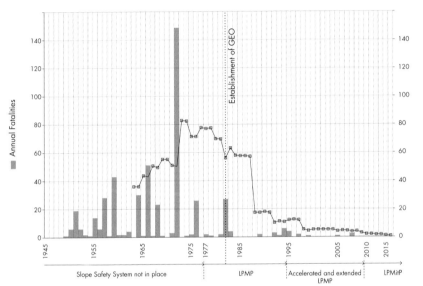

Figure 4. Landslide risk based on annual landslide fatalities in Hong Kong
Note: Redrawn from H.N. Wong (2017)

Figure 5. Major types of retaining walls and reinforcement options (page 29)
Note: Diagrams re-drawn from a wide range of documents, including
GEO (1996). GEO Report No. 31: Study of Old Masonry Retaining Walls in Hong Kong
GEO (2011). GEO Report No. 257: Study on Masonry Walls with Trees
GEO (2017). Geoguide 1: Guide to Retaining Wall Design
            (Amendment No. GG1/01/2017)
GEO (2017). Geoguide 7: Guide to Soil Nail. Design and Construction

a. Masonry Retaining Walls

a.1 Leaning Wall - opposite sides equal & parallel lean or slope 1/5 of height

a.2 Sloping Wall - slope in front 1/5 of height

a.3 Counter Sloping Wall - slope in rear 1/5 of height

a.4 Rectangular Wall

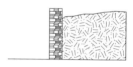

Rubble Stone Wall

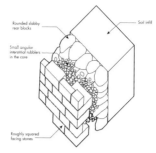

Rounded slabby rear blocks

Soil infill

Small angular interstitial rubblers in the core

Roughly squared facing stones

Walling Pattern

Tied-Face Wall

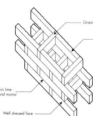

Granite ties

Rear blocks roughly defined undressed

Thin lime sand mortar

Well dressed face

Box-Bonded Masonry Wall

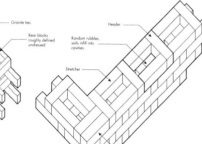

Header

Random rubbles, soils infill into cavities

Stretcher

Stone strips laid on edge

b. Gravity Retaining Walls

b.1 Mass Concrete Wall

b.2 Crib Wall

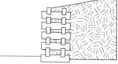

b.3 Gabion Wall

Closed-Faced Walling System

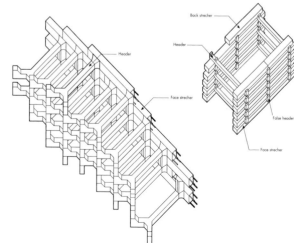

Header

Face strecher

Open-Faced Walling System

Back strecher

Header

False header

Face strecher

c. Reinforced Concrete Retaining Walls

c.1 R.C. L-/Inverted T-shaped Cantilever Retaining Wall

L-shaped   Inverted T-shaped

c.2 R.C. Counterfort Retaining Wall

Reversed L-shaped Inverted T-shaped

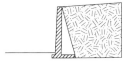

c.3 R.C. Buttressed Retaining Wall

with Counterforts   with Buttresses

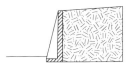

d. Improvement to Retaining Wall

d.1 Conventional Buttresses

d.2 Flying Buttresses

d.3 Soil-Nail Retaining Wall

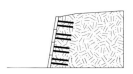
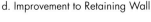

Exposed Isolated Soil-Nail Head Section

Hidden Isolated Soil-Nail Head Section

Typical Soil-Nail Retaining Wall Section

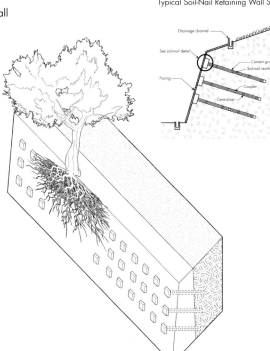

find a rectangular plate fixed to all slopes and retaining structures bearing the slope's unique registration number and the department responsible for its maintenance (Figure 3). These "identity cards" are a testament to four decades of efforts by the government to monitor and manage man-made slopes with a view to reducing landslide risks. In late 1976, a documentation of all man-made features that may constitute a risk to life should they fail was initiated. The first version of the *Catalogue of Slopes*, which was completed in 1978, provided details of approximately 10,000 slopes in the main urban areas of Hong Kong and Kowloon (Malone & Ho 1995). In 1998, the Systematic Identification and Registration of Slopes in the Territory project (SIRST), which aimed to document all sizeable man-made slopes in Hong Kong, was completed, containing 54,000 registered slopes (Chan 2000). The *Catalogue of Slopes* is regularly updated and today lists approximately 60,000 registered slopes (Choi & Cheung 2013).

Accompanying the documentation and monitoring process is a long-term systematic slope upgrading and retrofitting program known as the Landslip Preventive Measures Programme (LPMP), which was launched in 1976. In its first ten years, the LPMP focused mainly on the fill slopes associated with housing estates, schools and hospitals. By the mid-1980s, the proportion of soil cut slopes, rock cut slopes and retaining walls covered by the LPMP had increased, and a total of 620 slopes had been upgraded by 1994 (Choi & Cheung 2013). After another fatal landslide at Kwun Lung Lau in 1994,[5] the slope upgrading process was expanded, initially through the five-year Accelerated LPMP from 1995 to 2000, and later through the ten-year Extended LPMP from 2000 to 2010. A total of 3,714 slopes were upgraded from 1995 to 2010, and the landslide risk reached the "as low as reasonably practicable" level in 2010 (Chan 2011). The government has been implementing the Landslip Prevention and Mitigation Programme (LPMitP) since 2010 to dovetail with the expiry of the ten-year Extended LPMP. By September 2018, a total of 5,842 slopes had been upgraded by GEO through the LPMP and LPMitP (Civil Engineering and Development Department 2018) (Figure 4).

The design, construction and upgrading of man-made slopes have evolved over time with the technical advancements in slope engineering and construction techniques. The three main types of slopes of significant size that have been created since the late nineteenth century are fill slopes, soil-cut slopes and rock-cut slopes (Choi & Cheung 2013). In the case of retaining walls, the masonry construction approach was predominant prior to the mid-twentieth century, but was replaced in the post-war era by other construction materials and techniques, such as reinforced concrete, gravity (i.e., crib, gabion and mass concrete walls) and cantilevered retaining walls (Geotechnical Engineering Office 2017, 3). Prior to the 1990s, different upgrading techniques were applied to the various man-made slopes and retaining structures that involved extensive earthworks and vegetation clearance (Koirala & Tang 1988). The upgrading of fill slopes involved the excavation and re-compaction of the top layer of loose fill. Soil-cut slopes were upgraded by trimming back the slopes to a gentler profile. The design and extent of the necessary works to rock-cut slopes can only be finalized during the construction stage once a close inspection of the rock face can be made and after the true extent of the soft and hard material has been ascertained. Rock cutting, scaling, buttresses, dentition, dowels, rock bolts, additional drainage provisions and mesh netting are in common use as stabilization measures for rock cut slopes (Dubin, Watkins & Chang 1986). The masonry walls constructed between 1850 and 1950 in the region were a particularly important point of focus in the efforts to upgrade retaining structures, with stabilization measures including the provision of conventional or flying buttresses in front of the masonry wall, or the construction of hand-dug caissons behind the face of the wall (Wong & Jim 2011).

With the introduction of soil nailing techniques in the 1990s, the surface disruption required to achieve the objectives of the LPMP and LPMitP was decreased dramatically. Developed in the early 1960s and introduced to Hong Kong in the 1980s, soil nailing is used to improve the strength of soil masses involving the insertion of steel bars into deep pre-drilled grouted holes (Powell, Tang & Au-Yeung 1990). More adaptable to unforeseen weak geological and adverse groundwater conditions, soil nailing is also more cost-effective and robust than older methods. The technique also minimizes the impact on the existing vegetation cover, particularly on the existing mature trees that adorn the walls and slopes. The technique is particularly beneficial for the stabilization of old masonry retaining walls, especially those with banyan trees growing through the structure with aerial roots that extend across the surface of the wall. Soil nailing provides the obvious advantages of stability, while also preserving both the existing wall trees and the original masonry facade (Lui & Shiu 2005, 7) (Figure 5).

Figure 6. Examples of landscape treatments to man-made slopes (next page)
Note: Diagrams re-drawn from a wide range of documents, including
CEDD (1991). CEDD Drawing No. C2104/2: Tree Ring
CEDD (1991). CEDD Drawing No. C2001G: Concrete Planter Wall
CEDD (1994). CEDD Drawing No. C2007E: Granite Stone Planter Wall
CEDD (2002). CEDD Drawing No. C2507E: Planter Hole for Sprayed Concrete/
    Masonry Facing Slope
GEO (2011). GEO Publication No. 1/2011: Typical Planting Techniques for Slope Works

a. Guidelines for Planting on Slopes

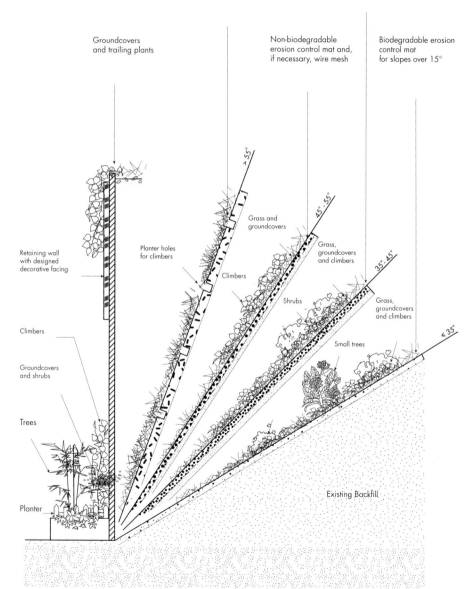

Hard surfacing with planter holes for climbers or mulching systems

Biodegradable or non-biodegradable erosion control mat

Groundcovers and trailing plants

Non-biodegradable erosion control mat and, if necessary, wire mesh

Biodegradable erosion control mat for slopes over 15°

Retaining wall with designed decorative facing

Planter holes for climbers

Grass and groundcovers

Grass, groundcovers and climbers

Climbers

Shrubs

Grass, groundcovers and climbers

Climbers

Small trees

Groundcovers and shrubs

Trees

Planter

Existing Backfill

> 55°

45° - 55°

35°- 45°

≤ 35°

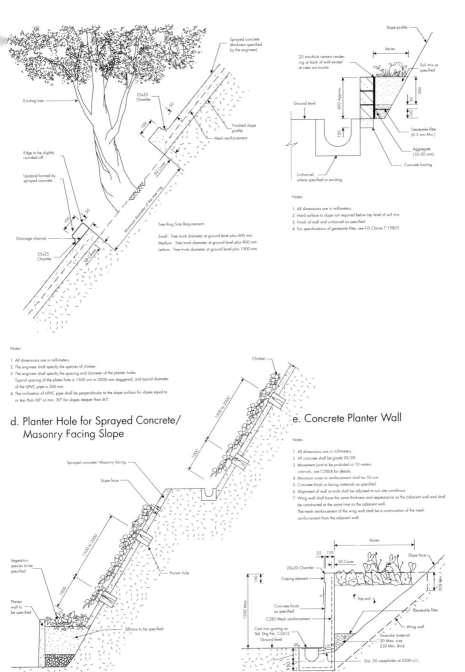

b. Section of Tree Ring

Sprayed concrete (thickness specified by the engineer)

Existing tree

25x25 Chamfer

50

100

Finished slope profile

Mesh reinforcement

50 Cover

Edge to be slightly rounded off

Upstand formed by sprayed concrete

Minimum diameter of the tree ring

Drainage channel

25x25 Chamfer

50 Cover

100 50

Tree Ring Size Requirement:

Small : Tree trunk diameter at ground level plus 600 mm
Medium : Tree trunk diameter at ground level plus 800 mm
Ledium : Tree trunk diameter at ground level plus 1000 mm

c. Granite Stone Planter Wall

Slope profile

Varies

20 mm-thick cement rendering at back of wall except at rake out mortar

Soil mix as specified

Ground level

450 Approx

300

50

100

100

U-channel, where specified or existing

Geotextile filter (0.5 mm Min.)

Aggregate (10-20 mm)

Concrete footing

Notes:

1. All dimensions are in millimeters.
2. Hard surface to slope not required below top level of soil mix.
3. Finish of wall and u-channel as specified.
4. For specifications of geotextile filter, see GS Clause 7.198(7).

Notes:

1. All dimensions are in millimeters.
2. The engineer shall specify the species of climber.
3. The engineer shall specify the spacing and diameter of the planter holes.
   Typical spacing of the planter hole is 1500 mm to 2000 mm staggered, and typical diameter of the UPVC pipe is 300 mm.
4. The inclination of UPVC pipe shall be perpendicular to the slope surface for slopes equal to or less than 60° or min. 30° for slopes steeper than 60°.

Climber

1500 to 2000

1000

d. Planter Hole for Sprayed Concrete/ Masonry Facing Slope

Sprayed concrete/ Masonry facing

Slope face

1500 to 2000

1000

Vegetation species to be specified

Planter hole

Planter wall to be specified

S6 mix to be specified

e. Concrete Planter Wall

Notes:

1. All dimensions are in millimeters.
2. All concrete shall be grade 20/20.
3. Movement joint to be probided at 10 meters intervals, see C2004 for details.
4. Minimum cover to reinforcement shall be 50 mm.
5. Concrete finish or facing materials as specified.
6. Alignment of wall at ends shall be adjusted to suit site conditions.
7. Wing wall shall have the same thickness and appearance as the adjacent wall and shall be constructed at the same time as the adjacent wall.
   The mesh reinforcement of the wing wall shall be a continuation of the mesh reinforcement from the adjacent wall.

Varies

Slope face

25 150

150

50 Cover

20x20 Chamfer

Coping element

300 Min.

Top soil

Concrete finish as specified

C283 Mesh reinforcement

1200 Max

Geotextile filter

Wing wall

Cast iron grating as Std. Drg No. C2412

Ground level

150

Granular material 20 Max. size 230 Min. thick

Dia. 50 weepholes at 2500 c/c

600 min.

33

Along with the application of more advanced geoengineering techniques like soil nailing, a number of landscape treatments and bioengineering measures have been developed and applied for aesthetic and ecological purposes. For example, localized retaining walls or tree rings have been designed to enable the retention of existing trees, while tree protection zones and/or protective wrapping around tree trunks serve to protect existing trees during construction works (Geotechnical Engineering Office 2012, 12). Collaborative works by engineers and landscape architects since the 1980s have progressively reduced the impact of slope works on the existing vegetation, and have resulted in design approaches that have substantially improved the greening of newly constructed and existing slopes, resulting eventually in the GEO publication *Technical Guidelines on Landscape Treatment for Slopes* in 2011. In modern slope designs and the upgrading of existing slopes, it is presumed that vegetation cover will be provided or retained unless it is impracticable to do so. In addition to planting directly onto soil-cut and fill slopes, other strategies include the terracing of rock slopes and the retention of structures to provide the space and soil volume for planting, and the establishment of climbing plants and screen planting in "toe-planters" to the bases of slopes.

Species are carefully selected for slope upgrading projects to achieve the desired ecological and bioengineering effects, with the use of native species encouraged so as to attract local wildlife, including birds and insects, which can then act as seed dispersers, thus enriching plant biodiversity (Geotechnical Engineering Office 2012, 8). The species that are most commonly planted on the walls and retaining structures in Hong Kong include such self-clinging climbers as the creeping fig (*Ficus pumila*) and diverse-leaved creeper (*Parthenocissus dalzielii*), while those that are most commonly planted on fill and soil-cut slopes include such groundcover as the oriental blechnum (*Blechnum orientale*) and the dichotomy forked fern (*Dicranopteris pedata*), along with shrubs and small trees like the blood-red melastoma (*Melastoma sanguineum*), the Chinese privet (*Ligustrum sinense*) and the Hong Kong gordonia (*Polyspora axillaris*). Ground cover species such as grasses and ferns protect the slopes from surface erosion, while others with deep root systems are used in bioengineering to stabilize slopes. There have been several trials aiming to integrate established engineering practices with ecological principles on Hong Kong's man-made slopes to provide mechanical, hydrological and environmental benefits (Geotechnical Engineering Office 2011, 50). For example, a program for the planting of deep-rooting vetiver grass has been launched to reinforce upgraded shotcrete cut slopes, and bamboo is also being planted strategically along drainage lines to restrict the passage of channelized debris flow (Figure 6).

Conclusion

The unique geography of Hong Kong and the efforts to manipulate this terrain for the needs of a high-density city are a counterpoint to the widely held narrative of the city's economically driven construction. This article presents an overview of the long-term efforts to stabilize Hong Kong's unconsolidated terrain, with the aim being to better understand the scale, materiality and spatial distribution of such small public spaces as Sitting-out Areas and Rest Gardens. With land being so scarce and valuable in Hong Kong, public amenities such as running paths, pocket gardens and bus stations are often skillfully integrated into the fragmented areas of land, cheek by jowl with the ubiquitous engineered slopes. Many of these small public spaces are living reminders of the ever-changing techniques of geoengineering and bioengineering that have shaped the existing urban configuration (Figure 7). The remarkably intimate relationship between the "hardness" of the man-made infrastructure and the "softness" of the ground below it, and of the vegetation that constantly attempts to engulf it, is taken for granted in this city. Here it is perfectly normal to stand next to a century-old masonry retaining wall, festooned in Chinese banyan roots, while waiting for a bus, or to jog along a hillside trail next to an almost-vertical fern-clad rock slope with climbing plants clambering through wire mesh. Waiting to pick up the children after school in a Sitting-out Area surrounded by concrete walls, but at the same time shaded by leafy woodland trees growing out of concrete "tree rings" is an everyday experience. Public access stairways, restricted slope maintenance staircases, cat ladders, site furnishings and amenities, pergolas and playground slides are interspersed with chunam slopes and stepped stormwater "U" channels.

The creation of Hong Kong has depended on a simultaneous process of leveling and retaining, resulting in an intimate and complex relationship between the existing, new and old ground conditions. The ongoing creation of new man-made slopes and the implementation of the slope upgrading program since the late 1970s continues to transform the ground of the city. Given that the risk of landslides can never be completely eliminated in Hong Kong, slope stabilization and maintenance measures are, and will continue to be, indispensable components of the city's civic space. Hong Kong's ground blurs the boundary between man-made and natural, between hard and soft, and between foreseeable and contingent, providing a unique point of reference in the discourse of public space within cities that in the future will have to grapple with overpopulation, tolerate extreme vagaries of climate and lack a natural *terra firma*.

Figure 7. Small public spaces as living archives of the ever-changing techniques of slope stabilization in Hong Kong: Wing Lee Street Rest Garden
Note: See pp. 202–205 in this volume

References

Bobbette, A. 2016. Contortions of the unconsolidated: Hong Kong, landslides and the production of urban grounds. *City* 20(4), 523–538.

Chan, R.K.S. 2000. Hong Kong Slope Safety Management System. *Proceedings of the Symposium on Slope Hazards and Their Prevention*, Hong Kong: 1–16.

Chan, R.K.S. 2011. Evolution of LPM Policy in the Past Thirty-Five Years. *Proceedings of the 31st HKIE Geotechnical Division Annual Seminar*, Hong Kong: 10–23.

Choi, K.Y., and Raymond W.M. Cheung. 2013. Landslide disaster prevention and mitigation through works in Hong Kong. *Journal of Rock Mechanics and Geotechnical Engineering* 5 (5): 354–365.

Civil Engineering and Development Department. 2018. *Achievements of the Geotechnical Engineering Office on Landslip Prevention and Mitigation*. Retrieved from https://www.cedd.gov.hk/eng/achievements/geotechnical/preventive/index.html. (Accessed January 15, 2019).

Dubin, B.I., A.T. Watkins and D.C.H. Chang. 1986. Stabilisation of existing rock faces in urban areas of Hong Kong. *Proceedings of the Conference on Rock Engineering and Excavation in an Urban Environment*. Hong Kong: The Hong Kong Institution of Engineers: 155–171.

Fan, Shuh Ching. 1974. *The Population of Hong Kong*. Hong Kong: C.I.C.R.E.D.

Frampton, Adam, Jonathan D. Solomon and Clara Wong. 2012. *Cities Without Ground: A Hong Kong Guidebook*. New York: Oro editions.

Geotechnical Engineering Office. 2011. *Technical Guidelines on Landscape Treatment for Slopes* (GEO Publication No. 1/2011). Hong Kong: Civil Engineering and Development Department.

Geotechnical Engineering Office. 2012. *Layman's Guide to Landscape Treatment of Slopes and Retaining Walls*. Hong Kong: Civil Engineering and Development Department.

Geotechnical Engineering Office. 2013. *When Hillsides Collapse – A Century of Landslides in Hong Kong*. Hong Kong: Civil Engineering and Development Department.

Geotechnical Engineering Office. 2017. *Guide to Retaining Wall Design* (Geoguide No. 1). Hong Kong: Civil Engineering and Development Department.

Hong Kong. 1977. *Report on the Slope Failures at Sau Mau Ping, August 1976*. Hong Kong: Government Printers.

Kingsmill, Thomas W. 1865. Article IX: Retrospect of events in China and Japan during the year 1865. *Journal of the North China Branch of the Royal Asiatic Society*, New Series no. II (December): 134–170.

Knill, J., P. Lumb, S. Mackey, V.F.B de Mello, N.R. Morgenstern, and B. G Richards. 1999. *Report of the Independent Review Panel on Fill Slopes* (GEO Report No. 86). Hong Kong: Geotechnical Engineering Office.

Koirala, N.P., and K.Y. Tang. 1988. Design of landslip preventive works for cut slopes in Hong Kong. *Proceedings of the Fifth International Symposium on Landslides*. Lausanne, Switzerland: 933–938.

Lui, B.L.S., and Y.K. Shiu. 2005. *Prescriptive Soil Nail Design for Concrete and Masonry Retaining Walls* (GEO Report No. 165). Hong Kong: Geotechnical Engineering Office.

Malone, Andrew, and Ken Ho. 1995. Learning from landslip disasters in Hong Kong. *Built Environment* 21 (2): 126–144.

Powell, G.E., K.W. Tang and Y.S. Au-Yeung. 1990. The use of large diameter piles in landslip prevention in Hong Kong. *Proceedings of the 10th Southeast Asian Geotechnical Conference*: 197–202.

Skertchly, Sydney B. J. 1893. *Our Island: A Naturalist's Description of Hong Kong*. Hong Kong: Kelly & Walsh Limited.

Town Planning Division. 1984. *Town Planning in Hong Kong*. Hong Kong: Town Planning Division, Lands Department.

Wong, C.M., and C.Y. Jim. 2011. *Study on Masonry Walls with Trees* (GEO Report No. 257). Hong Kong: Geotechnical Engineering Office.

Between the In-between: Research Findings on Data-Driven Strategic Urban Design

Alain Chiaradia and Lingzhu Zhang

Introduction

Pocket parks constitute a characteristic feature of Hong Kong's peculiarly dense high-rise urban typology, products of its compact development pattern, its planning regulations and open space standards.[1] What would elsewhere be forgotten areas or spaces (Lynch 1960; Trancik 1986), border vacuums (Jacobs 1961), cracks in the city (Loukaitou-Sideris 1996) or even *terrain vague* (Solà-Morales 1995), are co-opted as Sitting-out Areas or Rest Gardens in this jam-packed urban conglomeration. These seemingly accidental sites, the outcomes of providence, author a new script of urban chance encounters, of in-between spaces hidden in the city. A network of streets, steps and footpaths as well as indoor and outdoor elevated and underground walkways connect Hong Kong's public open spaces to their surrounding neighborhoods. Given such a complex multi-level city environment, can computational methods reveal hidden patterns in the allocation and planning of these interstitial spaces? Would a systematic exploration of the pedestrian network with the aid of artificially intelligent "agents," enabled with simplified human route choice preferences reveal its intangible secrets (Shatu, Yigitcanlar & Bunker 2019)? By interconnecting each interstice to every other and recording the resulting spider's web of meanderings, we hope to shed light on the configuration of the spatial cognitive map skeleton for these "between the in-between spaces" (Kuipers, Tecuci & Stankiewicz 2003). Is there a logical but hidden pedestrian network?

This chapter investigates the relationships between the spatial and other attributes of Sitting-out Areas (including Rest Gardens) in the Central & Western and Wan Chai Districts in Hong Kong. A citywide open space opinion survey, a three-dimensional spatial network analysis and a machine learning automated classification system were used to investigate the characteristics of the urban areas and how Sitting-out Area size, location visibility and design quality interact. Size and location are found to be significant factors along with accessibility and design quality. These findings lead to the drafting of a design brief for

[1] The standards for Open Space provision in Hong Kong are as follows: District Open Space 1 sqm per person, Local Open Space 1 sqm per person in residential areas and 0.5 sqm per person in commercial areas.

Figure 1. Sheung Wan to Wan Chai, Hong Kong Island: x-Ray 3D view of the outdoor and indoor pedestrian network (Chiaradia et al. 2018)

a proposed "cool network" system of shaded corridors linking these open spaces to the most frequented daily pedestrian routes, with the objective of enhancing the co-presence of all age groups.

Open Space Opinion Survey

In early 2018, independent Hong Kong public-policy think tank Civic Exchange conducted a public opinion survey of 3,600 Hong Kong residents across 18 districts on the quality of public open space (Lai 2018).[2] The survey revealed that small playgrounds or Sitting-out Areas in Hong Kong are the most frequently visited types of open space with 73% of respondents saying they visited these small public spaces at least three times a year.[3] Such a high frequency of visits to these small playgrounds or Sitting-out Areas was unexpected given the universality of shopping malls and public housing estates, the "staples" of Hong Kong's urban form. An analysis of the opinion survey by age group showed that the frequency of visits by older respondents (60–70+ years old) to small playgrounds, Sitting-out Areas and public housing open space was almost double the average. This appears to reflect Hong Kong's ageing demographic and their preferences. In contrast, the frequency of visits to plazas or podium gardens in shopping malls is almost the same for all age groups from 29–70+ but for the 16–29 age group the visit frequency to these spaces is nearly twice that of the others. All respondents recognized the importance of open spaces for fitness, stress relief, social life and as part of a daily walking routine (Lai 2018). How these different open spaces are located in relation to their users' walking patterns is of interest to planners and urban designers. Users may encounter these open spaces on their way to work, to school, or just incidentally in their neighborhood within their network of daily journeys. In all these instances, the open spaces have an impact on the informal encounters that contribute to social life in the city (Hillier & Hanson 1984; Shen 2019).

Overall, the opinion survey suggests a spatial-functional trend that can be referred to as the size, accessibility, visitor frequency function (Chow 2018, 60–61). Characteristically the smaller the open space and the denser its surroundings, making it more accessible to a larger population, the higher the frequency of visits. Usually the dwell-time in small open spaces is lower than in medium and large open spaces. Medium-sized and large parks that tend to be further away from home and therefore less accessible have a lower frequency of visits but a longer dwell-time as they provide a greater range of facilities and activities. While 97% of respondents reported visiting "open spaces" within walking distance from home, only 15%

[2] The survey was conducted between January and February 2018. The goal of this public opinion survey is to develop evidence-based recommendations to inform policies on the planning, design and management of open space as envisioned in "Hong Kong 2030+: Towards a Planning Vision and Strategy Transcending 2030."

[3] The large country parks of Hong Kong were excluded from this opinion survey.

did so from work or school (Lai 2018). The interplay of open space size, the frequency of visits by age bracket and the location of open spaces within users' daily route networks is investigated from the point of view of spatial accessibility and focuses on three particular questions. Firstly, what are the catchment areas of the open spaces given the importance of Sitting-out Areas as social foci in an ageing society? Secondly, are Sitting-out Areas in fact located on most people's daily routes? Finally, what are the implications of the accessibility or remoteness of an open space for its design quality?

Overcoming Limitations: (re)Evaluating, (re)Classifying, (re)Connecting

Here we acknowledge a key limitation of the opinion survey: the use of straight-line distance as a criterion for accessibility to and from the Sitting-out Areas. Straight-line distances do not consider the reality of street layouts or detours made necessary by obstructions to pedestrian movement such as major roads, topography or bodies of water. To calculate actual walking distances more accurately, we use a detailed three-dimensional pedestrian route-map as our network base. In addition to streets and footpaths, the walking network in Hong Kong includes public footbridges, steps and underpasses, and semi-public walkways within buildings and transport facilities such as Mass Transit Railway station concourses. Proximity dimension measurements are re-assessed using the pedestrian route-map, and alternative routes are compared. These findings inspired the idea of drawing up a design brief for a cool network of pedestrian connections to and from the open spaces. This study focuses on Sitting-out Areas and Rest Gardens in the Central & Western and Wan Chai Districts on Hong Kong Island (Figure 1). The Civic Exchange survey, which covered all Hong Kong's urban districts, reports that respondents from these Districts were the least satisfied with the quantity and quality of their open spaces.[4]

This investigation has three stages. Firstly, the straight-line criterion proximity index is compared to several variants of the pedestrian network map, including the complete three-dimensional pedestrian network revealing how much the straight-line criterion proximity index overestimates accessibility in the study area (Figure 2, 3). Secondly, an alternative methodology is proposed that takes account of proximity not just as a measured horizontal dimension but also as a matter of spatial cognition and spatial navigation in this complex, multi-level environment. Thirdly, we use unsupervised machine learning to automatically classify the Sitting-out Areas according to their attributes including size and proximity to user

[4] In the public opinion survey carried out by the Civic Exchange, respondents were asked to score their satisfaction with the quality of open space on a scale of 0 to 10. In general, respondents were moderately satisfied with the quality of open space in their communities, returning a median score of 6 out of 10 for most aspects such as quantity, greening, activities, and facilities. Residents in Central and Western returned a score of 5.2, in Wan Chai, 5.0 and in Yau Tsim Mong 5.1 – all showing significantly less satisfaction than the median.

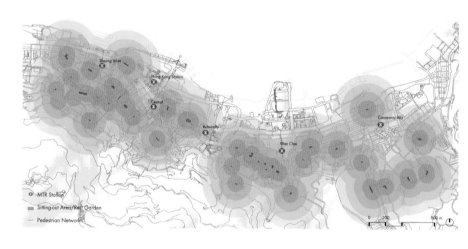

Figure 2. (top) Sitting-out Area catchments, with 0–100 m, 100–200 m, 200–300 m, and 300–400 m offsets shown in decreasing shade of green

Figure 3. (next page) Walking distance to Sitting-out Areas, with 0–100 m, 100–200 m, 200–300 m, and 300–400 m shown in decreasing shade of green; Figure 3a. Road center line network (A) (HKSAR 2018); Figure 3b. Outdoor path center-line pedestrian network (B) (Sun et al. 2018) and Figure 3c: Outdoor + Indoor path center-line pedestrian network (C) (Chiaradia et al. 2018). The difference between A and B is clearly visible, while the difference between B and C is not

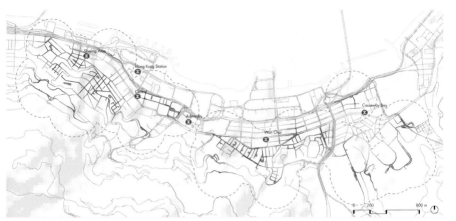

Figure 3a

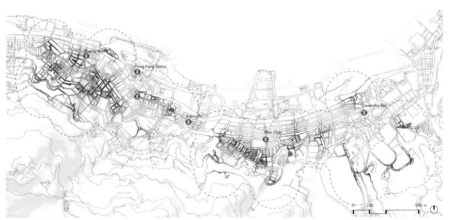

Figure 3b

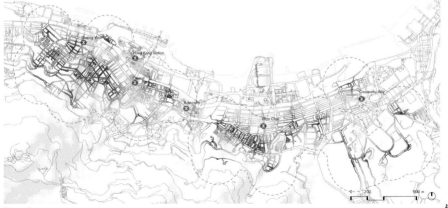

Figure 3c

catchment areas and surrounding pedestrian flows. The classification results are crosschecked against a design quality score based on onsite assessments (Figures 4–9). The machine classification results indicate whether design quality is related to visibility to residents or people working in the area. Consistent with Jane Jacobs' hypothesis (Jacobs 1961) that pedestrian flows are equivalent to "eyes on the street" we find that the visibility of a Sitting-out Areas does indeed impact its design quality.

Finally, we draft an evidence-based design brief for Wan Chai District (Figures 9, 10) based on the findings above. This suggests that Sitting-out Areas connected by a cool network of shaded corridors are most likely to be used, not only by the Sitting-out Area users we would normally expect to find there, but also by most people living, working and visiting the area, especially if the cool network coincides with the most frequently used daily pedestrian routes.

From 2D to 3D: (re)Evaluating Proximity to the Sitting-out Areas

The simplest way of measuring accessibility to the open spaces is by use of a proximity index, a circular catchment determined by straight-line (as the crow flies) measurements centered on the open space itself. Figure 2 shows a series of circular catchment areas measured from the entrances of each of the Sitting-out Areas located from Sheung Wan to Causeway Bay.[5] The opinion survey indicates that there are a sufficient number of Sitting-out Areas in these areas. Combining the catchments that have a maximum radius of 300 m, two aggregations are recognizable. One grouping covers the area from Sheung Wan to Central and is bunched together, forming a circuit of sorts. The second grouping, from Admiralty to Causeway Bay, is linear and meandering.

[5] On flat terrain, 400 m of walking distance equals to 5 minutes of walking.

A people-centered approach entails consideration of the built environment and the street layout. In most cities, motor vehicle traffic lanes and pedestrian footpaths are generally parallel and share the same street courses, meaning the road center-line representation is a good proxy of pedestrian circulation. This is not the case for this study area. While the walking realm is planar and two-dimensional in most cities, in this study area it is three-dimensional. As a pedestrian one may proceed straight on, turn left or right, or return, but one may also climb or descend, up and down a myriad of stairs, escalators, lifts, slopes and steps, some public and some semi-public, some indoors and some outdoors. Figure 3a shows the road centerline network as a proxy for the outdoor pedestrian-path network at street-level. Figure 3b shows the same outdoor network with the addition of public footbridges and pedestrian only paths. Figure 3c shows the same pedestrian-path network as shown in figure 3b with the addition of publicly accessible indoor walkways at ground level, above and below ground.

Table 1 compares the various approaches to measuring proximity to and from Sitting-out Areas. It shows that the proximity of Sitting-out Areas can be seriously under or overestimated according to the Level of Definition (LOD) of the pedestrian network; from straight-line (A), to road centerline (B), to outdoor pedestrian network (C), to outdoor and indoor pedestrian network (D).

pedestrian network level of definition	(A) straight-line catchment	(B) 2D road network centreline as pedestrian network proxy; network (B) based catchment	(C) complete 3D outdoor only pedestrian network; network (C) based catchment	(D) complete 3D outdoor & indoor pedestrian network; network (D) based catchment
(A) straight-line catchment	N/A			(A) underestimates the proximity of SOAs by 70% on average, ≈ +91 km, compared to (D)
(B) 2D road network centreline as pedestrian network proxy; network (B) based catchment		N/A	(B) underestimates the proximity of SOAs by 17% on average, ≈ -9 km, compared to (C)	(B) underestimates the proximity of SOAs by 33% on average, ≈ -18 km, compared to (D)
(C) complete 3D outdoor only pedestrian network; network (C) based catchment			N/A	(C) underestimates the proximity of SOAs by 8% on average, ≈ -10 km, compared to (D)
(D) complete 3D outdoor & indoor pedestrian network; network (D) based catchment				N/A

Table 1. The table summarizes the impact of the interaction between Pedestrian Network Level of Definition and proximity to Sitting-out Areas

The comparison demonstrates that pedestrian proximity to amenities such as Sitting-out Areas analyzed using straight-line or road centerline definitions is extremely inaccurate in these Hong Kong districts. The straight-line definition results in an overestimate of 70% and the road centerline an underestimate of up to 33%. A comparison of catchment areas as defined by the complete three-dimensional outdoor-only pedestrian network definition and the complete three-dimensional outdoor and indoor pedestrian network definition results in a small difference in length of 8% on average. It should be noted however that this 8% differential is made up of key pedestrian connections between the outdoor pedestrian network and the heavily used indoor pedestrian network (Zhang & Chiaradia 2019).

This shows that the omission of an apparently small amount of data, as represented by the indoor pedestrian network can dramatically prejudice the proximity analysis. The indoor pedestrian network is relatively small in length compared to the outdoor network, yet in Hong Kong it is extremely heavily used and must be included in any proximity analysis.

With the outdoor and indoor pedestrian networks included, we can now proceed with investigating our hypothesis that "eyes on" these Sitting-out Areas do result in better spaces. We investigate the idea that Sitting-out Areas as "between spaces" are made better by virtue of being more visible, because they are in-between the origins and destinations of a large number of pedestrian journeys and consequently are found on the regular daily routes of a bigger proportion of the population.

Unsupervised Machine Learning: (re)Classifying the Sitting-out Areas

Figures 4 and 5 represent the simulated relative potential pedestrian flow derived from artificially "walking" the three-dimensional outdoor and indoor pedestrian network based on a catchment of 400 m from any given point on the pedestrian network. The "walks" are undertaken following a simplified route choice preference approach, seeking the shortest and most direct connections (Golledge 1999; Montello 1998; Shatu, Yigitcanlar, & Bunker 2019). The red pedestrian links are those where the most direct connections overlap, and where the highest pedestrian flows may logically be predicted. Figures 4 and 5 show the predicted flow peaks centered on Central, Admiralty and Wan Chai MTR stations.

The Sitting-out Areas were automatically classified by an unsupervised machine learning program that identifies similarities and distinctiveness in the data, analyses the results based on the presence or absence of common characteristics and sorts the Areas into groups (groups 1–4). The attributes of each individual Sitting-out Area are determined; these include size, accessibility in terms of predicted adjacent pedestrian flow, a "quality score" and the jobs-to-housing ratio for the surrounding area. In terms of size, the Sitting-out Areas range from 11 to 1410 sqm. The level of accessibility or predicted adjacent pedestrian flow is calculated based on the proximity index including the entire outdoor and indoor pedestrian network.

Theoretical Flow Potential Analysis
High
Low

Figure 4

Theoretical Flow Potential Analysis
High   Low

Figure 5

Figure 4. (top) Sheung Wan to Causeway Bay, Hong Kong Island: Plan view, 400 m
potential pedestrian flow level (Red – high. Dark blue – low) based on the 3D outdoor and
indoor pedestrian network using sDNA (Chiaradia, Crispin & Webster 2012)
Figure 5. (bottom) Wan Chai to Sheung Wan, Hong Kong Island: 3D view, 400 m potential
pedestrian flow level (Red – high, Dark blue – low) based on the 3D outdoor and indoor
pedestrian network

The "quality score" rating takes into account the salient attributes of urban green spaces in high-density cities (Wan & Shen 2015) including themed design, sculpture, placement of seating, vegetation and the extent to which spatial design takes advantage of uniqueness of context. Each Sitting-out Area was rated by three assessors on a scale ranging between "most beautiful" (scoring +3) and "least beautiful" (scoring -3), their three ratings then being amalgamated and confirmed by majority vote.

The jobs-to-housing ratio is the ratio of jobs to residents in a given area. This can be deduced from detailed information about numbers of residents and workplaces available for the various urban Districts in question. The ratio of working people to residents is especially relevant in the case of Central where the resident population is so small and the working population so large that using residential density alone would result in a drastically skewed picture of user presence.

The dendrogram result shown in Figure 6-1 shows the four distinct groups of Sitting-out Areas classified by size and accessibility. Figure 6-2 shows the individual computer-generated Sitting-out Areas in their respective groups and Figure 7 shows them mapped in context. The majority of the Sitting-out Areas are in Group 1 (34%) and Group 4 (47%), with the outliers represented by Groups 2 (11%) and 3 (8%).

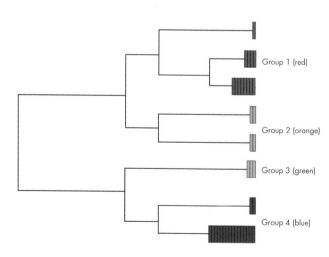

Group 1 (red)

Group 2 (orange)

Group 3 (green)

Group 4 (blue)

Figure 6-1. (top) Sitting-out Areas in their computer-generated groups
Figure 6-2. (next page) Unsupervised machine learning cluster analysis, grouped by size, quality, accessibility, proximity to other Sitting-out Areas and jobs-to-housing ratios

Group 1

(Size: 371 to 1,411 sqm)

1.
Lambeth Walk Rest Garden
(2.33)

2.
Queen Street Rest Garden
(4.67)

3.
Lun Fat Street Rest Garden
(2.67)

4.
Lok Hing Lane Temporary Sitting-out Area
(3.67)

5.
Wing Lee Street Rest Garden
(2)

6.
Wong Nai Chung Road Rest Garden
(3.67)

7.
Wing Lee Street Sitting-out Area
(2.33)

8.
Wa On Lane Sitting-out Area
(3)

9.
Spring Garden Lane Sitting-out Area
(3.33)

10.
Broadwood Road Rest Garden
(3)

11.
Tung Lo Wan Road Sitting-out Area
(3.67)

12.
Ceverly Street Sitting-out Area
(3.67)

13.
Amoy Street Sitting-out Area
(3.67)

Group 2

(Size: 137 to 482 sqm)

17.
Graham Street Sitting-out Area
(3)

18.
Queen's Road East/Swatow Street Sitting-out Area (1.33)

19.
Cochrane Street Sitting-out Area
(3.67)

20.
Chater Road Sitting-out Area
(3.67)

Group 3

(Size: 137 to 432 sqm)

14.
Eastern Hospital Road Sitting-out Area
(3.67)

15.
Eastern Hospital Road Temp Rest Garden
(3.33)

16.
Gloucester Road/Cannon Street Sitting-out Area
(2.33)

Group 4

(Size: 11 to 370 sqm)

21.
Pier Road Sitting-out Area
(2.67)

22.
Kennedy Street Sitting-out Area
(2.67)

23.
Hennessy Road/Johnston Road Sitting-out Area (1)

24.
Tai Wong Street East Sitting-out Area
(2.33)

25.
Wing Ning Street Sitting-out Area
(3)

26.
Lower Albert Road Sitting-out Area
(1.33)

27.
Queen's Road East/Hennessy Road Sitting-out Area (2.33)

28.
Bullock Lane Road Sitting-out Area
(2)

29.
Wong Nai Chung Road Sitting-out Area
(1.33)

30.
Robinson Road/Seymour Road Sitting-out Area (2.33)

31.
Bowen Road Temporary Sitting-out Area
(2.67)

32.
Lun Fat Street Sitting-out Area
(2)

33.
Lan Kwai Fong Sitting-out Area
(2.33)

34.
Bonham Road Rest Garden
(2.67)

35.
Upper Station Sitting-out Area
(3)

36.
Chung Wo Lane Sitting-out Area
(1)

37.
Monmouth Terrace Sitting-out Area
(2.33)

38.
Robinson Road Sitting-out Area
(1)

Group 1 (Red) are large sized, high quality, highly accessible, in just below median proximity to other Sitting-out Areas and mostly in areas with high jobs-to-housing ratios. In contrast, Group 4 (Blue) are small sized, low quality, not very accessible, in just above median proximity to other Sitting-out Areas and mostly in areas with low jobs-to-housing ratios. The outliers in Group 2 (Orange) and Group 3 (Green) are all medium sized and high quality. Group 2 are highly accessible while Group 3 are inaccessible. Group 2 are in median proximity to other Sitting-out Areas, while Group 3 are remote. Group 2 are in areas with high jobs-to-housing ratios, while Group 3 are in areas with low jobs-to-housing ratios.

Other observations related to Groups 1–4 are summarized as follows:
- Sitting-out Areas in Group 1 (Red) are located between Sheung Wan and Causeway Bay. They are mostly on the fringes of the areas with high jobs-to-housing ratios. They are generally larger in size, highly visible and of good quality.
- Sitting-out Areas in Group 2 (Orange) are located around Soho and Central with one in Wan Chai. They are highly visible and of good quality.
- Sitting-out Areas in Group 3 (Green) are bigger than most in the other groups and are located in Causeway Bay and Happy Valley. They are visible and of good quality.
- Sitting-out Areas in Group 4 (Blue) are relatively small, located mainly in residential areas, not very visible and of lower quality.

These computer-generated groups corroborate Jacobs' hypothesis that the more "eyes on" a Sitting-out Area, the better quality it is likely to be. Group 1 displays a correlation between larger size; accessible and visible location; and good quality. The sizes of the Group 1 Sitting-out Areas allow for better quality design. Their locations, adjacent to high predicted pedestrian flows in areas with high proportions of jobs-to-housing, means they are seen by large numbers of residents and working people. The contrast between highly visible, high quality Sitting-out Areas with close proximity to workplaces, and their poorly visible and low quality counterparts in residential areas, suggests why residents express dissatisfaction with the provision of open space in these districts. These findings raise the question as to the optimum location for Sitting-out Areas – should they be provided in the middle of residential areas invisible to most "outsiders," or should they be located as interfaces between areas with differing characteristics (Mehaffy et al. 2010).

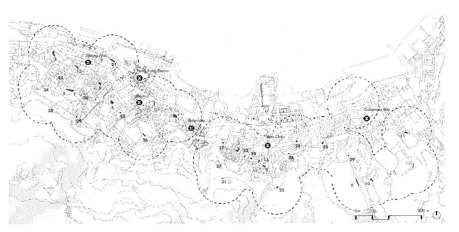

Figure 7. Sheung Wan to Causeway Bay, Hong Kong Island: Unsupervised machine learning cluster analysis, Group 1 (Red), 2 (Orange), 3 (Green), 4 (Blue), location and size

Group 1
Lambeth Walk Rest Garden

Group 1
Tung Lo Wan Road Sitting-out Area

Group 2
Queen's Road East/Swatow Street
Sitting-out Area

Group 2
Chater Road Sitting-out Area

Group 2
Cochrane Street Sitting-out Area

Group 3
Eastern Hospital Road Sitting-out Area

Group 3
Gloucester Road/Cannon Street Sitting-out
Area

Group 4
Chung Wo Lane Sitting-out Area

Group 4
Bowen Road Temporary Sitting-out Area

Group 4
Monmouth Terrace Sitting-out Area

Between the In-between Spaces: (re)Connecting Public Spaces in Wan Chai

In this section, the quantitative and qualitative data-driven findings explained above are employed to formulate a design proposal. A wealth of research testifies to the beneficial effects of public open space in urban areas. In this context, Hong Kong has invested in Sitting-out Areas including exercise facilities for older people. When asked about the importance of open space in their daily lives, respondents of all age groups rated fitness as the most important benefit, stress relief second, social life third, followed by how well the open space was integrated with the user's daily journeys (Lai 2018, 120). As seen above, although good design and accessibility are not necessarily coordinated in these informal spaces, they do provide venues for older people to meet, socialize, exercise, and rest. The findings make a case for integrating the locations of Sitting-out Areas with the most frequently used pedestrian routes. A program of integrating Sitting-out Areas and medium and large open spaces with a shaded pedestrian network linking shopping malls, urban plazas and waterfront promenades would improve the environment for all user types, of all ages. Figure 9 shows the locations of open spaces, commercial centers and the waterfront promenade in Wan Chai, while the most frequently used daily pedestrian routes are shown in Figure 10 (Zhang & Chiaradia 2019). Wan Chai District has a population of about 180,000; one-third residential, and the rest workers. Approximately 20% of the residential population are over 60 years of age, but no age information is available on the workplace population. A cool network as described above would permit the elderly population to walk to and from Sitting-out Areas on their daily routes through indoor air-conditioned spaces, particularly during Hong Kong's exceedingly hot and humid summers. This interconnected cool network would provide socio-economic, health and environmental benefits. The provision of additional planting to complement the existing disposition of trees, particularly along those parts of the pedestrian network with the highest predicted pedestrian flow (Figure 10), would maximize the health and environmental benefits. The Sitting-out Areas would then be interconnected by a network incorporating air-conditioned, publicly accessible indoor spaces, thereby optimizing the amount of additional shading required.

Figure 8. (previous page) Photos of Sitting-out Areas for each group identified by unsupervised machine learning

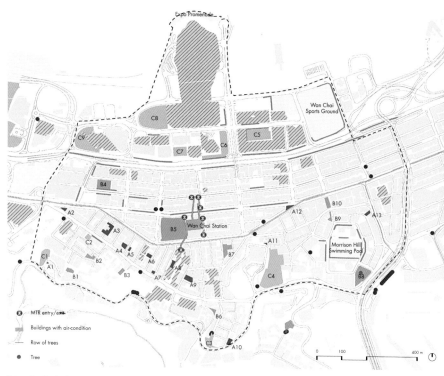

Sitting-out Area/Rest Garden

A1: Monmouth Terrace Sitting-out Area
A2: Queen's Road East/
Hennessy Road Sitting-out Area
A3: Li Chit Street Sitting-out Area
A4: Lun Fat Street Rest Garden
A5: Lun Fat Street Sitting-out Area
A6: Tai Wong Street East Sitting-out Area
A7: Queen's Road East/
Swatow Street Sitting-out Area
A8: Amoy Street Sitting-out Area
A9: Spring Garden Lane Sitting-out Area
A10: Kennedy Street Sitting-out Area
A11: Bullock Lane Sitting-out Area
A12: Hennessy Road/Johnston Road Sitting-out Area
A13: Wing Ning Street Sitting-out Area

Playground

B1: Monmouth Terrace Playground
B2: Kwong Ming Street Children's Playground
B3: Ship Street Playground
B4: Lockhart Road Playground
B5: Southorn Playground
B6: Wan Chai Gap Road Playground
B7: Tai Wo Street Playground
B8: Stubbs Road Children's Playground
B9: Tak Yan Street Children's Playground
B10: Hennessy Road Playground

Park/Garden

C1: Monmouth Park
C2: Dominion Garden
C3: Stone Nullah Lane Garden
C4: Wan Chai Park
C5: Harbour Road Garden
C6: Central Plaza Garden
C7: Gloucester Road Garden
C8: Hyatt Hotel Garden
C9: The Academy Garden

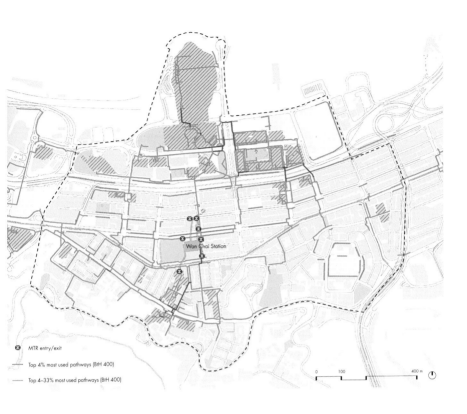

⊗   MTR entry/exit

——   Top 4% most used pathways (BtH 400)

——   Top 4–33% most used pathways (BtH 400)

Wan Chai Station

0   100   400 m

Figure 9. (previous page) Wan Chai District, Hong Kong Island, showing Sitting-out Areas and other medium parks, open spaces and playgrounds. The hatched areas show publicly accessible air-conditioned buildings/places. Green lines denote rows of trees, and dark green denotes individual trees registered as old and valuable trees.

Note: Several spaces are excluded, such as Wanchai Sports Ground and Morrison Hill Swimming Pool, which are not publicly accessible at all times. The Expo Promenade is considered a special case.

Figure 10. (top) Wan Chai District, Hong Kong Island, showing the 33% most frequently used pedestrian routes. Combined with Figure 9 this facilitates the selection of routes for incorporation into the cool network, i.e., shaded connections that would link all the open spaces.

Research on Urban Design, Informing Urban Design Sketching

This study interrogates the fitness for purpose of the straight-line distance indicator as a criterion for measuring accessibility of open spaces in Hong Kong. A city with such a multi-layered access network and ambiguous definition of "openness" as Hong Kong, requires indicators that take these complexities into account, combining pedestrian network distance and cognitive distance to interpret the built environment for all in an intelligible way (Marquardt, Bueter & Motzek 2014). The straight-line distance criterion is widely used in the evaluation and assessment of social, spatial structures and their impact on wellbeing. The choice of method of measurement might appear to be an academic technical issue of little consequence, yet this study demonstrates that it has a large impact on the interpretation of the actual conditions that affect the elderly population, who are the primary users of Sitting-out Areas. In this case the choice of research technique is not neutral but an ethical issue (Sen 1997) affecting how the distribution of a public good is valued. Another problematic aspect of such techniques is that they are blind to design quality. While facilitating policy formulation (Lai 2018, 124–129), their use creates a rift between policy and design, because designers are unable to make use of a technique that cannot differentiate between effective and ineffective design, an issue usually overlooked by "spatial design-blind" research design.

In contrast, people-centered improvements to proximity measurements that account for both the measured geography of the pedestrian network map and cognitive accessibility measures allow better interconnectivity between policymaking and design. The route choice preference simulation integrates ways of measuring peoples' cognitive choice capabilities (Sen 1997) and their capacities to move physically and thoughtfully, taking their physical and psychological preferences and health into account. Finally, we add a "ground truth" in the form of intersubjective qualities such as "aesthetics" to the evaluation of the Sitting-out Areas. Urban Design research tends to shy away from these inevitably subjective, humanistic evaluations.
The aim of this new approach is to account for both communality, or the "generalizable city" (Hillier & Hanson 1984), and the uniqueness of the Sitting-out Areas' constructed characteristics. This allows us to understand what is generalizable, such as how streets define accessibility as they do in any city, and what is unique to any given part of a city or type of urban layout. In Hong Kong's case, this approach allows a better understanding of the complexity of accessibility to specific features of the city leading to a logical approach to designing interventions. A simple machine learning

program was used to classify and bundle together Sitting-out Areas according to their diverse spatially quantitative and grounded qualitative attributes, revealing that Jacobs' "eyes on the street" hypothesis that the visibility of Sitting-out Areas is related to their design quality, appears to be valid in this case. This is however a theoretical proposition requiring further investigation.

This study's new approach also attempts to integrate various groups of people who typically have different preferences concerning "public" open space, yet who use the same daily routes to access them. In Central, preferences vary between workers and residents, yet all ages and occupation groups are potentially co-present in the same spaces. The cool network proposed between these in-between spaces, could provide more comfortable interconnectivity thereby enhancing the ecology and diversity of urban chance encounters in Hong Kong's sub-tropical high-rise concrete jungle.

All illustrations are from the authors unless otherwise stated. © 2018/19 HKU FoA DUPAD Thanks to Minyu Cui and Wenxin Zeng for their research assistance in preparing the data used in this project, and Wenxin Zeng for her assistance with translating the original manuscripts into Chinese.

References

Chiaradia, A., C. Crispin and C. Webster. 2012. sDNA a software for spatial design network analysis v01. Retrieved from https://www.cardiff.ac.uk/sdna/software/download/ (Accessed February 10, 2019).

Chiaradia, A., L. Zhang, S. Khakhar, X. Su, Y. Cui, J. Zhu and H. Tse. 2018. Walkable HK Central and Hong Kong, 3D indoor and outdoor pedestrian network. Hong Kong: University of Hong Kong, Faculty of Architecture, DUPAD. Funded by HKU grant.

Chow, J. 2018. Public open space accessibility in Hong Kong, a geospatial analysis. Hong Kong: Civic Exchange. Retrieved from https://civic-exchange.org/report/open-space-opinion-survey-full-report/ (Accessed February 10, 2019)

Golledge, R. G. 1999. Human wayfinding and cognitive maps. In *Wayfinding Behavior: Cognitive Mapping and Other Spatial Processes,* ed. R. G. Golledge. Baltimore: JHU Press. 5–45.

Hillier, B., and J. Hanson. 1984. *The Social Logic of Space.* Cambridge: Cambridge University Press.

HKSAR. 2018, 06 01. Road Network, Road centreline. From DATA.GOV.HK: https://data.gov.hk/en-data/dataset/hk-td-tis_6-road-network/resource/7863c98b-eff6-4842-a219-748769dcc803 (Accessed January 3, 2019).

Jacobs, J. 1961. *The Death and Life of Great American Cities.* New York, NY: Random House.

Kuipers, B., D. Tecuci and B. Stankiewicz. 2003. The skeleton in the cognitive map: A computational and empirical exploration. *Environment and Behavior* 35 (1): 81–106.

Lai, C. 2018. Open Space Opinion Survey (Full Report). Hong Kong: Civic Exchange. Retreived from https://civic-exchange.org/report/open-space-opinion-survey-full-report/ (Accessed February 10, 2019).

Loukaitou-Sideris, A. 1996. Cracks in the city: Addressing the constraints and potentials of urban design. *Journal of Urban Design* 1 (1): 91–103.

Lynch, K. 1960. *The Image of the City.* Cambridge (MA): MIT press.

Marquardt, G., K. Bueter and T. Motzek. 2014. Impact of the design of the built environment on people with dementia: An evidence-based review. *Health Environments Research & Design Journal* 8 (1): 127–157.

Mehaffy, M., S. Porta, Y. Rofe and N. Salingaros. 2010. Urban nuclei and the geometry of streets: The "emergent neighborhoods" model. *Urban Design International* 15 (1): 22–46.

Montello, D. R. 1998. A new framework for understanding the acquisition of spatial knowledge in large-scale environments. In *Spatial and Temporal Reasoning in Geographic Information Systems,* ed. M. J. Egenhofer and R. G. Golledge. Oxford: Oxford University Press. 143–154.

Sen, A. 1997. *Choice, Welfare and Measurement.* Cambridge, MA: Harvard University Press.

Shatu, F., T. Yigitcanlar and J. Bunker. 2019. Shortest path distance vs. least directional change: Empirical testing of space syntax and geographic theories concerning pedestrian route choice behaviour. *Journal of Transport Geography* 74: 37–52.

Shen, Y. 2019. Dynamic space syntax: Towards the configurational analysis of high frequency cities. *Urban Planning International* 34 (1): 54–63.

Solà-Morales, I. 1995. Terrain Vague. In *Anyplace* ed. C. Davidson. 118–123. Cambridge, MA: MIT Press.

Sun, H., C. Webster, X. Zhang and A. Chiaradia. 2018. Walkable HK, 3D enabled 2D outdoor pedestrian network of Hong Kong. Hong Kong: The University of Hong Kong, Faculty of Architecture.

Trancik, R. 1986. *Finding Lost Space: Theories of Urban Design*. New York, N.Y.: John Wiley & Sons.

Wan, C. and G. Shen. 2015. Salient attributes of urban green spaces in high density cities: The case of Hong Kong. *Habitat International* 49: 92–99.

Zhang, L. and A. Chiaradia. 2019. Three-dimensional spatial network analysis and its application in a high density city area, Central Hong Kong (In Chinese). *Urban Planning International* 33 (1): 46–53.

On Imported Planning Policies: Adaptability and Resilience of a Small Public Open Space Typology

Susanne Trumpf

Introduction

Sitting-out Areas and Rest Gardens in Hong Kong are seldom celebrated for their design or spatial qualities. If they catch any attention, it is more likely to be because of their uncomfortably pragmatic facilities, their bureaucratically anachronistic nomenclature or their long lists of prohibited activities. Their allocation, sometimes obvious, sometimes inexplicable, whether formal or informal, in old neighborhoods or government-planned housing estates, is a reflection of the city's diverse and ever-changing planning regulations over the past century.

This essay is an attempt to interpret the fragmented urban typologies of these Sitting-out Areas in relation to the large-scale planning strategies that spawned them. The examination of the stories and policies that lie behind the Sitting-out Areas, some unique and some typically representative, focuses on the Kowloon Peninsula – a conglomerate of old neighborhoods, satellite towns, industrial quarters and transport hubs that now includes a new Central Business District emerging in Kowloon East. It is of little relevance whether the district's planning strategies were large-scale or neighborhood oriented; government funded or privately initiated; widely adopted or just a forgotten experiment for a specific time and place. Even the humblest urban space within the district tells us something about the city's urban planning history and can offer us a glimpse into the potential future evolution of a public open-space typology recurring to be allocated with almost congruent appearance since the end of World War II.

Within the overall framework of land use policies and urban planning strategies today, Sitting-out Areas and Rest Gardens languish at the bottom of the priority list. Usually measuring less than half a hectare and classified as a Local Open Space, these areas are viewed as minor planning incidents rather than part of a network of intentionally planned open spaces. Despite the recreational value they hold for their immediate neighborhoods, their classification as a

Passive Open Space has bequeathed them far fewer guidelines and standards than those that exist for the Active Open Space, which includes larger recreational amenities such as sports grounds and district or town parks (Planning Department 2015).

The *Hong Kong Planning Standards and Guidelines* dating back to 1982, were the first official standards for the provision of recreational space set up to ensure "appropriate public facilities to meet the needs of the public." Originally a government manual for internal use, these standards and guidelines were made publicly accessible in 1991. Chapter 4 of the guidelines, addressing "recreation, open space and greening" remains the city's only relevant recommendations on open space provision, which despite lacking the force of law, represents a milestone in the context of the city's extreme urban density.

City, Congestion and Exploratories

The typology of Sitting-out Areas emerged in the context of the rapid urbanization of Hong Kong after World War II and can be seen as a by-product of attempts to transplant British town planning theory to this Asian city. This was despite British planning experts acknowledging, in the 1940s, that the majority of Britain's town planning principles were difficult to adapt to their colonial city's hilly topography and limited land resources. Just after World War II, Sir Patrick Abercrombie, well known for his post-war holistic planning proposals for London, addressed several ideas for the provision of recreational grounds in his *Hong Kong Preliminary Planning Report* in 1948. His predictions for the land use potential for urban recreational grounds are a remarkably close match to the different allocation categories we see in Hong Kong today. His analysis of Hong Kong's urban condition suggested making use of leftover spaces, which were unsuitable for the types of land use that required larger scale lots. He suggested, for example, using hillside slopes for open spaces "before more land is leased for suburban or quasi-suburban building" (Abercrombie 1948).

Planning decisions prior to Abercrombie's recommendations had been made on an ad-hoc basis. The city's earliest urban open spaces were a response to overcrowding and poor sanitation. Blake Garden in Tai Ping Shan, is one of the first public open spaces in Hong Kong. It was established at the end of the nineteenth century to help reduce population density, after an epidemic of bubonic plague struck the congested urban areas of Sheung Wan in the west of the City of Victoria. Blake Garden still stands today – an example of a pioneering strategy of replacing formerly built-up blocks with open space to promote a healthier, less densely populated and more hygienic neighborhood environment.

Strategic responses to the problems of an increasingly congested city continued as Hong Kong expanded. Greenfield sites were developed on the periphery of the built-up core areas, and in the 1920s and 30s small-scale, fully planned neighborhoods like Kowloon Tong sprang up, inspired by the British Garden City movement. The layout of the low-density suburban-looking Kowloon Tong owes much to Ebenezer Howard's famous concentric diagrams describing an organized city layout with open spaces and boulevards. Today, two of the smaller open space segments are public pleasure grounds under the management of the Leisure and Cultural Service Department. The Essex Crescent Rest Garden,[1] gazetted as a public open space in 1963, features a plaque commemorating Montague Ede, a businessman who founded the Kowloon Tong Estate in 1922. Streets with low-rise villas surround this radially shaped piece of land with dense tree cover reaching out to the adjacent private gardens. This garden, and its smaller counterpart Dorset Crescent Rest Garden, remain the only examples of this small open space typology in the area (Figure 1). The majority of the other open spaces nearby exceed the maximum half-hectare that is typical of a Sitting-out Area. To this day, the provision of Countable Open Space in Kowloon Tong of 7.7 sqm per person is outstandingly generous by Hong Kong standards, far exceeding that of the nearby inner urban areas of Kowloon (Lai 2017). [2]

While density and overcrowding have been persistent factors throughout the city's development, it was not until after World War II that policies were initiated on a territory-wide scale to reduce congestion. Even though building legislation existed as early as the mid-nineteenth century, the *Building Ordinance,* as we know it today was only established in 1955. It prescribes maximum building heights, open space provision and plot ratios. The *Density Zoning Policy* which followed in 1965, uses three levels of density in the urbanized areas to categorize land use from "main urban areas" (Zone 1) and "suburban residential neighborhoods" (Zone 2) to "more remote parts" (Zone 3) (Town Planning Division 1984).[3] Once in place, these policies took time to achieve their intended results, and meanwhile the city sought to tackle its overcrowding problems by controlling and limiting informal and illegal developments. The Yau Ma Tei Community Centre Rest Garden is one example.[4] Originally, the front court of Tin Hau Temple was densely populated with *dai pai dong* (cooked food stalls) (Figure 2). These were demolished between 1963 and 1968 (Hong Kong Memory Project 2011), and today this space, canopied by large banyan trees, is one of the

[1] See pp. 126–129 in this volume.

[2] Criteria for *Countable Open Space* are defined by the *Hong Kong Planning Standards and Guidelines* and refer to location (mostly in urban areas), qualities and accessibility.

[3] The *Density Zoning Policy* is part of the *Town Planning Ordinance.*

[4] See pp. 130–133 in this volume.

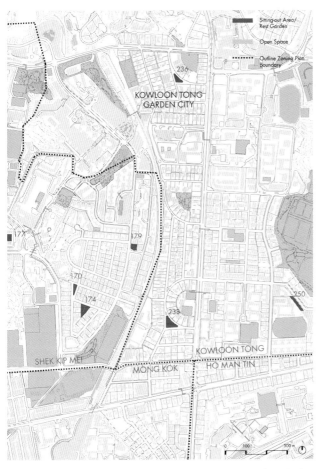

Figure 1. Open space map of Kowloon Tong showing Sitting-out Areas and Rest Gardens with area reference of Kowloon Tong Garden City Estate as originally planned in 1922 and Outline Zoning Plan nos. S/K18/21 (Kowloon Tong), S/K7/24 (Ho Man Tin), S/K3/31(Mong Kok) and S/K4/29 (Shek Kip Mei)

Note: All identification numbers on the maps in this chapter refer to the index of Sitting-out Areas and Rest Gardens on pp. 118–119

Figure 2. Tin Hau Temple, Yau Ma Tei, 1968. The image shows part of the front court which is today transformed into a Rest Garden (image reproduced with permission of the Hong Kong Special Administrative Region Government, Information Services Photo Library).

most active public spaces in the neighborhood. Even though the *dai pai dong* were never re-established, the square retains an air of informality. During the day it forms the front court for visitors to the adjacent Tin Hau Temple, which lends its name to the famous Temple Street night market. At night, the market extends into the Rest Garden and vendors spread out their diverse products across the square. Occasionally, musical performers entertain passers-by and the Rest Garden is frequented by any number of jacks-of-all-trades, with a plethora of unauthorized activities in what is normally a highly regulated public space. The *Pleasure Grounds Regulation* strictly limits what is allowed in such spaces, and hawking, cycling or playing music are just a few on a long list of prohibited activities (Department of Justice of the Government 2018).

There are 26 Rest Gardens within the mere 40-hectare area between Yau Ma Tei and Mong Kok (Figure 3). The area has one of the densest clusters of Sitting-out Areas and Rest Gardens within a single neighborhood and Yau Ma Tei Community Centre Rest Garden is the largest of these. The overwhelming presence of this particular typology is evidence of a policy that dates to the 1970s. In 1974, the Town Planning Office undertook an assessment of the environmental quality of residential districts in the main urban areas.[5] In this study, Mong Kok, Yau Ma Tei, Sham Shui Po, To Kwa Wan, and Ngau Chi Wan in Kowloon, and Sai Ying Pun and Wan Chai on Hong Kong Island were identified as old and environmentally poor neighborhoods, sorely lacking in recreational and community facilities (Town Planning Division 1984). The typology of the Sitting-out Area became a ready tool for the administration to increase the open space provision in the late 1970s and early 1980s. Local newspaper and media coverage dating back to that time includes numerous articles on the newly constructed Sitting-out Areas, located mostly in those areas the report had identified as environmentally poor.

[5] In 1989, the Planning Department emerged from the Town Planning Office as an independent department (Lai 2000).

Land, Reclamation and Industries

The city's primary response to the problem of increasing density, however, was land reclamation on a massive scale. This was already underway when Abercrombie wrote his report, and he took into account planned land reclamation as a means to produce a new crop of much needed open space in the future. While open space provision was not a significant objective for the early reclamation areas – built primarily to cater for growing commercial, residential and industrial land uses – over one third of the Sitting-out Areas and Rest Gardens on the Kowloon Peninsula today are in fact located on reclaimed land.

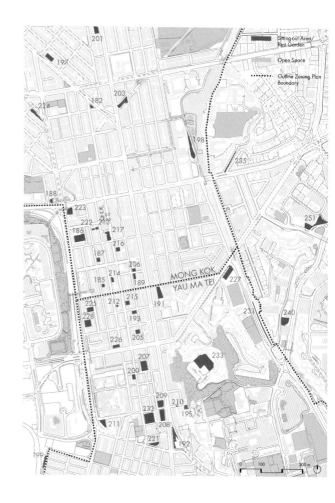

Figure 3. (top) Open space map of Yau Ma Tei and Mong Kok showing Sitting-out Areas and Rest Gardens with area references to Outline Zoning Plan nos. S/K3/31 (Mong Kok) and S/K2/22 (Yau Ma Tei)

Figure 4. (next page) Open space map of Kowloon Bay (and North Point on Hong Kong Island) showing Sitting-out Areas and Rest Gardens with area references to historical land reclamation and Outline Zoning Plan nos. S/K22/6 (Kai Tak), S/K14S/22 (Kwun Tong South) and S/K13/29 (Ngau Tau Kok & Kowloon Bay)

NGAU TAU KOK & KOWLOON BAY

KAI TAK

KWUN TONG (SOUTH)

The 1921 *Annual Administrative Report* stated that in addition to land reclamation, extensive garden lots had been built over, on the Kowloon Peninsula, to satisfy the increasing demand for land development (Bristow 1984). The reclamation of Kowloon Bay in the 1920s was one of the largest such schemes to date. The size of the bay was reduced further when more land was reclaimed for the expansion of Kai Tak Airport; for the nearby industrial areas of To Kwa Wan and Kwun Tong in the 1950s and 1960s; and finally for the urban area called Kowloon Bay in the 1980s (Figure 4).

The urban configuration of Kowloon Bay, still dominated by industrial buildings, allows for just a few intricate and fragmented leftover areas of land. Yet still, Sitting-out Areas have been squeezed into the narrow corridors between the large industrial blocks. For example, four linear open spaces (the Sitting-out Areas of Kai Cheung Road, Lam Hing Street,[6] Wang Tai Road and Lam Fook Street) form an intermediary buffer between the areas of Kowloon Bay and Kwun Tong. This strip of land, between just four and eight meters wide, consists of a long thin corridor sandwiched between large planters, creating a surprisingly lush experience and screening the unpleasant backwalls of the adjacent industrial buildings. Together, these Sitting-out Areas have a significant impact on the urban environment with their uniform earth-tone-tiled planters stretching almost 400 m across several city blocks (Figure 5).

[6] See pp. 246–249 in this volume.

Several other Sitting-out Areas were introduced along the edge of areas that were reclaimed later, located opposite the former Kai Tak Airport runway. The Hoi Bun Road Sitting-out Area for example,[7] built by the Urban Council in 1982, had an unobstructed view of the runway where visitors could admire the spectacular sight of aircraft landing against the backdrop of the famous Hong Kong skyline.[8] This view was framed by the elevated Kwun Tong bypass, a remarkable piece of engineered infrastructure constructed in the 1980s and positioned just in front of the Hoi Bun Road Sitting-out Area. Since the relocation of the airport to Chek Lap Kok on another large land reclamation just north of Lantau Island, East Kowloon has undergone a dramatic transformation. Energizing Kowloon East, a government initiative aimed at revitalizing the former Kai Tak Airport site, the Kwun Tong Business Area and the Kowloon Bay Business Area, has opened up the old Kwun Tong dockside, which is now a public park on the waterfront. This prestigious new promenade has absorbed the Hoi Bun Road Sitting-out Area and incorporated it into its new design language (Figure 6, 7).

[7] See pp. 220–223 in this volume.

[8] The Urban Council was responsible for municipal services in Hong Kong Island and Kowloon until the handover in 1997.

Environmentalists and planning experts have argued for an increase in the open space provision for many years (Jim 1994), and in 2002

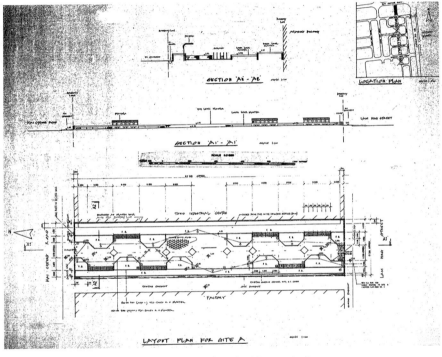

Figure 5. Landscaping at Kowloon Bay Amenity Strips (Kai Cheung Road Sitting-out Area) Layout plan & sections, 1990 (Reproduced with permission of Architectural Services Department)

Figure 6-1. (top) Hoi Bun Road Sitting-out Area before the renovation 2013
(image source: Creative Commons by Zhungkeiwaiskalc, licensed under CC BY-SA 3.0)
Figure 6-2. (bottom) Hoi Bun Road Sitting-out Area, 2019
Figure 7-1.(next page, top) Hoi Bun Road Sitting-out Area, New Layout Plan and Sections, 1999 (Reproduced with permission of Architectural Services Department)
Figure 7-2. (next page, bottom) Refurbishment of Hoi Bun Road Sitting-out Area, General Layout, 2014 (Reproduced with permission of Architectural Services Department)

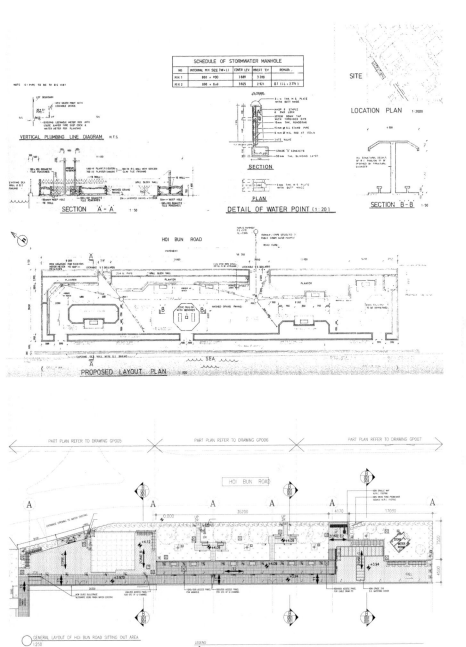

SCHEDULE OF STORMWATER MANHOLE

NO	INTERNAL M.H. SIZE [W×L]	COVER LEV	INVERT LEV	REMARK
M.H 1	800 × 900	3.889	3.299	
M.H 2	800 × 800	3.925	2.921	D.I (I.L + 2.771)

NOTE : D.I PIPE TO BE TO B.S 1387

VERTICAL PLUMBING LINE DIAGRAM N.T.S.

SECTION 'A-A' 1:50

SECTION

PLAN

DETAIL OF WATER POINT (1:20)

SITE

LOCATION PLAN 1:2000

SECTION 'B-B' 1:50

HOI BUN ROAD

PROPOSED LAYOUT PLAN 1:100

SEA

PART PLAN REFER TO DRAWING GP005   PART PLAN REFER TO DRAWING GP006   PART PLAN REFER TO DRAWING GP007

HOI BUN ROAD

GENERAL LAYOUT OF HOI BUN ROAD SITTING OUT AREA
1:250

LEGEND

REMARK: ALL RC FOOTING DESIGN REFER TO STRUCTURAL DRAWING

the government updated the *Planning Standards and Guidelines*, to increase the recommended amount of open space per person from 1.5 to 2 sqm in residential areas. The recommended provision of open space in industrial and commercial areas, however, has remained at 0.5 sqm per worker since the guidelines were first promulgated in 1982. This means that Kowloon East's shifting land use from predominantly industrial to commercial would have little impact on its open space provision, although some prestigious government projects such as the Zero Carbon Building and open spaces incorporated in new private developments have made significant recent contributions.[9]

Country, Parks and Authorities

Hong Kong's notoriously bureaucratic and complex array of government departments dissect the public realm into many different planning, funding, design, management and maintenance responsibilities, making the process of implementing new Sitting-out Areas and Rest Gardens rather opaque. These can appear and disappear within the city's constant hubbub of demolition and construction, apparently without notice. Their low construction cost and relatively uncomplicated maintenance makes them susceptible to quick conversion when the land uses change. The sudden transformation of a playground into a Sitting-out Area at Poplar Street for example, was announced in the South China Morning Post in 1983. The site was to be handed over from the Lands Office to the Highways Office to allow for the construction of a new flyover along Cheung Sha Wan Road.[10] In the meantime, the site would be developed into a "Sitting-out Area with some planting" by the Urban Services Department (SCMP 1983).[11]

On a larger scale, the process of transferring Sitting-out Areas and Rest Gardens to different management authorities caters to the altering requirements of open space. In 2007, for example, 170 sites formerly developed and managed by the Home Affairs Department, were transferred to the Leisure and Cultural Services Department under the District Council Review (Chan 2018). Today, the Leisure and Cultural Services Department manages all public open space facilities and oversees the maintenance of over 500 Sitting-out Areas and Rest Gardens.

Without any specific requirements or guidelines on the provision of Sitting-out Areas and Rest Gardens, their allocation mirrors the story of the city's statutory planning frameworks. The first *Town Planning Ordinance* was enacted in 1939 and led to the drafting of *Outline Zoning Plans* for the urban areas.[12] In 1976, the *Country*

[9] The first zero carbon building in Hong Kong, developed by the Construction Industry Council, is located in Kowloon Bay and was completed in 2012. In addition to highly sophisticated unique buildings promoting a resourceful city, the government increasingly advocates for Public Open Space in Private Developments (POSPD). The Development Bureau published specific *Design and Management Guidelines* in 2008.

[10] Lands Offices operate on a district level and are overseen by the Lands Department. The Lands Department is responsible for all land matters in Hong Kong, including land disposal and acquisition as well as the maintenance of man-made slopes (Lands Department 2019). The Highways Department, the authority responsible today, was established in 1986 and evolved from the Highways Office of the former Engineering Development Department (Highways Department 2019).

[11] The Urban Services Department was the executive branch of the Urban Council and was abolished following the handover. Its responsibilities regarding public open space were transferred to Leisure and Cultural Services Department.

[12] The *Outline Zoning Plans* (OZP) show the proposed land-uses and major road systems of individual planning scheme areas. Areas covered by such plans are zoned for such uses as residential, commercial, industrial, open space, government, institution or community uses, green belt, conservation areas, comprehensive development areas, village type development, open storage or other specified purposes.

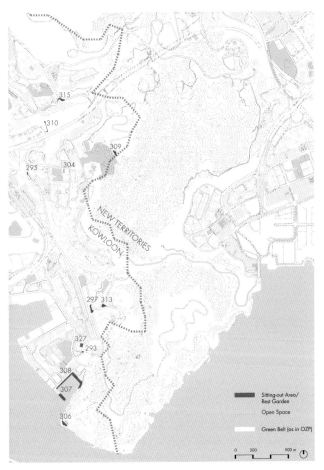

Figure 8. Open space map of the area around Ma Yau Tong/Black Hill showing Sitting-out Areas and Rest Gardens with references to Green Belt as defined in Outline Zoning Plan nos. S/K15/25 (Cha Kwo Ling, Yau Tong, Lei Yue Mun) and S/TKO/26 (Tseung Kwan O)

Sitting-out Area/
Rest Garden

Open Space

Green Belt (as in OZP)

0   300   900 m

Parks Ordinance was enacted, another major component of modern statutory planning in Hong Kong. Initiated by a report conducted by Dr. Lee Talbot, an ecologist and conservation expert in the 1960s, it led to the Country Parks being established for "open air recreation" and "protection of the countryside" (Cheung 2016). Country parks and green belts are counted as Regional Open Space and are not included in the required open space provision under the *Hong Kong Planning Standards and Guidelines.* But Sitting-out Areas are frequently encountered along the urban fringes, and between the urban areas and the country parks. They mostly provide some benches and hard landscaping from which to enjoy the wider scenery beyond. Locating Sitting-out Areas within, adjacent or in close proximity to larger scale parks or country parks is a recurring strategy to allocate new Local Open Space (Figure 8).

The Ma Yau Tong Central Sitting-out Area is located just adjacent to the larger Lam Tin Park, along Black Hill, at the periphery of Kwun Tong.[13] The area, classified as a Green Belt in the *Outline Zoning Plan,* is a former landfill site that allows for very limited construction. The Ma Yau Tong Central Sitting-out Area was completed in 2010 along with the Ma Yau Tong West Sitting-out Area in the more urbanized part of Lam Tin, as part of a new government program launched in 2008. The *District Minor Works Programme* homepage announces these new open spaces of approximately 1000 sqm and meticulously lists all its facilities. The four sets of elderly fitness equipment and eight arbors – each approximately two meters long with a bench, and fifteen other benches illustrate the type of basic facilities commonly provided in such public open spaces. The program, mainly aimed at upgrading street furniture such as planters, benches or rain shelters, also targets the provision of Local Open Space. It funds district-based work projects initiated by the District Councils to improve "local facilities, living environment and hygienic conditions" (District Minor Works Programme 2015). However generic, the program promises a more dedicated allocation of funds towards the implementation of small public spaces, but the allocation is at the discretion of local district councilors who may have other priorities. Since the launch of the program, a total of about 40 Sitting-out Areas have been installed or refurbished, of which nine are in Hong Kong Island and Kowloon.

It is usual practice for local district councilors to demand additional public open space within their district boundaries or to suggest specific sites. The Planning Department, which is responsible for implementing the statutory planning framework, rarely initiates the construction of a specific Sitting-out Area. Implementation is the responsibility of the Architectural Services Department, which acts

[13] See pp. 280–283 in this volume.

as the work agent of the Leisure and Cultural Services Department, resulting in a rather generic design language for Sitting-out Areas throughout the city.

Potentials and Procedures

Over the years, the provision of Sitting-out Areas and Rest Gardens has adapted to shifting regulations, different government policies and evolving planning standards. They are now well-established as generic but valuable recreational refuges in the dense urban areas of the city. Besides occupying underused land or temporarily filling in gaps which are subject to changes in land use, even the smallest spaces contribute towards meeting the modest open space provision of a minimum of 2 sqm per person in the urban areas. Within the government's *Planning Vision and Strategy* there are recommendations to upgrade the provision of open space slightly by 2030 to 2.5 sqm per person (Development Bureau and Planning Department 2007).

There has been little government pressure to tackle the lack of local open space, but in recent years an increasing range of concern groups and neighborhood advocacy groups have taken up the issue of the shortage of public space and the protection of local heritage sites. Yet planning on a neighborhood scale remains a challenge. A fully public participatory approach has never been formally adopted and the decision-making processes around the implementation and design related to these areas is undertaken in-house by the government. Sitting-out Areas and Rest Gardens are rarely tendered out to private design companies unless there is a personnel shortage within government departments. The requirements for approved consultants are inflexible and only a few firms are invited to tender.[14] Larger consultancies show a limited interest in committing to such small-scale design projects that call for complex innovative, site specific and community sensitive approaches.

Ground conditions in the densely built-up areas often involve a tangle of utilities, old or geotechnically suspect foundations, slopes and other infrastructure, along with problems of accessibility for construction, all of which complicate any design initiatives and predicate against anything but the most basic design solutions. The suggested 70% of soft landscaping for Passive Open Space comes with a number of possible exemptions including keeping penetrating roots several meters distant from water mains, drainage pipes, manholes and circulation routes, which makes greening a difficult

[14] Contracts can only be outsourced to consultants shortlisted on the Architectural and Associated Consultants Selection Board (AACSB). The list includes firms who meet certain criteria, such as having completed at least two projects with a budget of over 25 million HKD within the past five years (Architectural Service Department, 2018).

endeavor. As a result of all these factors, the relatively smaller Sitting-out Areas and Rest Gardens, that measure less than 500 sqm in area are dominated by hard landscaping and prefabricated site-furniture. Current guidelines for the planning and design of Sitting-out Areas and Rest Gardens are based on the large-scale two-dimensional statutory planning framework quite unfit for this purpose. They call for a design approach and organizational framework that can adapt to the diversity and uniqueness of the sites and their users' requirements. Abercrombie alludes to this type of approach in his 1948 report, suggesting that the design of what he called "Rest Parks" be related to their local context, going on to remark that the "particularly rocky ground [in Kowloon] lends itself to the Chinese type of romantic garden design" (1948). In the future, Sitting-out Areas and Rest Gardens in this dense and ever more built-up context will require a design and maintenance framework which is able to satisfy government requirements and local community aspirations, to respond to the unique and contradictory forms and functions of the urban core areas and urban fringe, and to be sensitive to the ecology of their site-specific flora, fauna and human beneficiaries.

References

Abercrombie, Patrick. 1948. *Hong Kong: Preliminary Planning Report.* Hong Kong: Ye Olde Printerie.

Architectural Service Department. 2018. *Minimum Entry Criteria for Consultants Lists: Landscape Architectural Consultants.* Retrieved from https://www.archsd.gov.hk/media/339761/la_rev26_.pdf (Accessed February 21, 2019).

Bristow, Roger. 1984. *Land-use Planning in Hong Kong: History, Policies and Procedures.* Hong Kong/Oxford: Oxford University Press.

Chan, Horman. 2018. Personal Communication (April 18).

Cheung, Chi-Fai. 2016. *Country Parks and Protected Areas in Hong Kong.* Retrieved from https://www.legco.gov.hk/research-publications/english/essentials-1617ise06-country-parks-and-protected-areas-in-hong-kong.htm (Accessed February 21, 2019).

Department of Justice of the Government. 2018. *Cap 132: Public Health and Municipal Services Ordinance, Part X: Pleasure Grounds Regulation.* Retrieved from: https://www.elegislation.gov.hk/hk/cap132!en?INDEX_CS=N&xpid=ID_1438402662604_002 (Accessed March 25, 2019).

Development Bureau and Planning Department. 2007. *Hong Kong 2030: Planning Vision and Strategy: Final Report.* Hong Kong: The Government Logistics Department.

Highways Department. 2019. *Organization: The Facts.* Retrieved from https://www.hyd.gov.hk/en/about_us/organisation/index.html (Accessed June 3, 2019).

Hong Kong Memory Project. 2011. *Opening Hours, Facilities and Foods of Dai Pai Dongs in Yau Ma Tei.* Retrieved from https://www.hkmemory.hk/collections/oral_history/All_Items_OH/oha_04/records/index.html#p48288 (Accessed February 21, 2019).

Iim, C.Y. 1994. Urban Renewal and Environmental Planning in Hong Kong. *The Environmentalist* 14 (3): 163–181.

Lai, Carine. 2017. Unopened Space: Mapping Equitable Availability of Open Space in Hong Kong. Hong Kong: Civic Exchange.

Lai, Lawrence W C, and Ki Fong. 2000. *Town Planning Practice: Context, Procedures and Statistics for Hong Kong.* Hong Kong: Hong Kong University Press.

Lands Department. 2019. Retrieved from https://www.landsd.gov.hk/en/about/welcome.htm (Accessed June 3, 2019).

Lau, Pei-Ping. 1983. Playground to become sitting out area. *South China Morning Post,* June 9.

Planning Department. 2015. *Hong Kong Planning Standards and Guidelines.* Hong Kong: The Government of the Hong Kong Special Administrative Region.

Ambiguous Topologies of Public Open Space in Hong Kong: Stairs, Alleyways, Sitting-out Areas, Parks, Playgrounds, Privately Owned Public Spaces and Vacant Lots

Melissa Cate Christ and Andrew Toland

Introduction

In the densely occupied, hilly urban areas of Hong Kong Island, public open space is limited and often fragmented. By necessity, these scarce spaces are multi-functional, resisting normative and typical categories of classification. Every in-between space that does exist is often a site of occupation, processes, flows, materials, wastes and daily routines that are undertaken by both human and non-human actors. These spaces comprise a complex, mostly contiguous, network of streets, alleys, stairs, plazas, parks, Sitting-out Areas, Rest Gardens, Children's Playgrounds, privately owned public spaces and passageways, overhead walkways, underground tunnels, terraces, planter beds, drainage channels and even vacant parcels of land. Of these spaces, only some are labeled and maintained by the government as public "open space." This latter type of official space, categorized as parks, children's playgrounds, Sitting-out Areas and Rest Gardens (the latter two being the focus of this publication), have signposted rules and sometimes full-time attendants and/or cameras to enforce what is allowed (or not) in these, often tiny, fragments of land. However, the practices in these spaces are not limited only to "allowed activities," and the allowed activities are not limited only to these spaces. In fact, some practices are common to all of the parts of the more loosely defined open space network mentioned above, whereas others seem to be more unique and localized.

It is often difficult to distinguish which type of space one is occupying through its formal classification alone. In such dense, over-built and often vertiginous conditions, spaces have a tendency both to bleed into one another, but also to be interrupted and disjoined in unexpected and surprising ways. Fully comprehending the ways in which human and non-human actors use, maintain and occupy this system requires an understanding of the complex connections between the spaces and the actors within those spaces, and their participation in both the local and wider open space network. This article explores the topology of these actors and sites within the larger network of public open space, highlighting the ambiguity of their formal classification, and focusing on the practices which connect or disconnect many of these sites.

"Topology" is a term that has recently been advanced in landscape architectural theory. It is intended to express the "physical and poetic reality of a landscape" in its "wholeness," as described by Christophe Girot (2013, 81). Its recent use in architectural disciplines has been inspired by developments in the computer sciences and investigations into complex geometries.[1] In earlier usages, in the nineteenth and early twentieth centuries, the term described the practice of a "scientific" study of a place (OED Online 2018). In the 1970s, the cultural geographer Yi-Fu Tuan proposed the neologism "topophilia" to describe humans' "affective ties with the material environment" (1974, 93). Both Girot's and Tuan's formulations contain a normative register and are also underpinned by a desire to seek out a unifying and coherent understanding of places and landscapes. The interest of this article in the urban landscapes of Hong Kong, however, is driven by the tendency of its open space network to resist such readings. Rather than wholeness, coherence or straightforward attachments to place, these urban spaces produce certain conditions of ambiguity across a range of analytical categories.

Particular aspects of Hong Kong – its brute materiality, its confounding architectural accretions, its defiance of easy interpretation – are reminiscent of Walter Benjamin and Asja Lacis's famous 1925 essay on Naples:

> Buildings and action interpenetrate in the courtyards, arcades, and stairways. In everything they preserve the scope to become a theater of new, unforeseen constellations. The stamp of the definitive is avoided. No situation appears intended forever, no figure asserts its "thus and not otherwise." (1978, 166)

Benjamin and Lacis's repeated motif is porosity: the porosity of the built urban fabric, of the life of the streets and of (not-so) private lives. Hong Kong can also be read as a porous city.[2] In a similar vein, Hong Kong author Dung Kai-Cheung's *Atlas: The Archaeology of an Imaginary City* (2012) is a fragmented "map" of the city, told, in part, through the "fragmented micro-history of Hong Kong local streets" (in the words of literary scholar Esther Cheung). As in Naples, this porosity is the product not just of the fragmentation and interpenetration of spaces and actors which exist in the present moment, but also of an ongoing negotiation with its past, and with a center of power that is always elsewhere (London, Beijing) (Cheung 2003, 606-607). Hong Kong's open space system is the

[1] These usages also emphasize properties of continuity, and hence also "wholeness" (Lynn 1993).

[2] Perhaps the most (in)famous site of porosity in Hong Kong – a city within a city – was the Kowloon Walled City, now demolished (Leung Ping Kwan 1998). Kowloon Walled City found its way into the postmodern imaginary like a version of Benjamin and Lacis's notion of Naples on speed – inspiring everything from Hollywood science fiction (most famously Blade Runner [1982]), to Japanese manga and anime, to international video games (Fraser & Cheuk-Yin 2017).

product of planning in only a minimal sense; mostly it is the result of accretion and retrofitting. In many ways, Hong Kong's streets can be interpreted as material forms that physically manifest the historical literary mode of *fangzhi* – traditional Chinese urban "gazetteers." This literary style is characterized by an amalgam of historical and topographical writing (topographical in the strict etymological sense of writing about a specific place), myths, gossip and socio-economic information. It is a mode that influenced contemporary Hong Kong writers in the years surrounding the Handover (Taylor 2003, 55 and 62–63), mixing intimacy and detachment, and combining minor registers with the grand sweep of historical events. These dynamics find expression in the material structures of the city itself; Hong Kong's global drive to consolidate its status as a "world city" generates a persistent interplay with more localizing and vernacularizing tendencies.

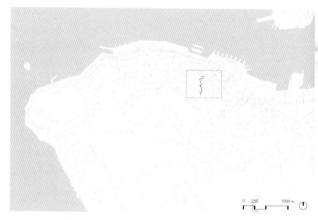

Figure 1. Area of the route

Some expatriate designers have also come to this realization: "The city's long and narrow lanes collect the overflow of the micro scale, the excesses, and because the spaces are not saturated with function, there is room for appropriation ... Appropriating a space is like feeling at home ..." (Borio & Wüthrich 2015, 78).

To discuss the role of porosity and ambiguity in stymying a topological reading of Hong Kong's open space network, this article highlights several conditions, instances and locations along a walking route in Hong Kong's Central District, namely from Caine Road to Queen's Road Central (Figure 1 and Figure 2).

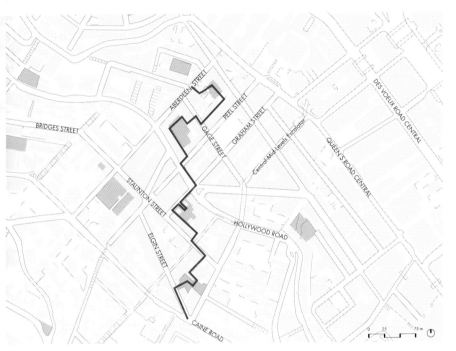

Figure 2. Route map

A Walking Tour

As one of the oldest colonially settled areas of the city, the street network laid out during the term of Hong Kong's first governor, Henry Pottinger, is still largely extant, with mostly British Colonial names for the main streets and Chinese names for the lanes and alleys. However, the grain and materiality of the built environment has substantially changed, turning over many times in most blocks and street frontages since the mid-nineteenth century. Due to this turnover leaving gaps, consolidating blocks or widening streets, the open space network not only consists of the primary street grid, but also sidewalks, setbacks, alleys, stairs, terraces and open spaces. Some of these spaces are identified through posted signs as parks, Sitting-out Areas, Rest Gardens, children's playgrounds, or privately owned public spaces – it can sometimes be difficult to tell them apart from a merely visual inspection without this declaratory signage. Other spaces are seemingly vacant, often enclosed by a dilapidated fence and most likely awaiting redevelopment or consolidation with other lots nearby. Nevertheless, these ostensibly vacant sites reward careful observation; it is possible to begin to pick out markers of occupation amongst the overgrown weeds – papaya trees, stashes of belongings, thrice-repaired furniture saved from the trash bin to make an informal seating area or mysterious collections of materials ready to be made use of by the surrounding community (Figure 3).

Other open spaces such as alleys and stairs also present themselves (particularly when one ventures off the main street grid) adjacent to or on the thresholds of named open spaces, or as seeming extensions of streets or sidewalks. Ownership boundaries, with or without posted signs rather than a fence or a wall, are sometimes indicated through a change in ground material. These include sharp lines between standard-issue, cast-in-place concrete and dimensional stone or concrete pavers, or a thin strip of metal edging which physically outlines the abstract cadastral property line. Both of these can demarcate the area required to be maintained by private owners rather than by government departments (Figure 4). More often though, it is the use (or misuse, in the owner's and manager's eyes) of these spaces that imply a boundary and that indicate the ambiguous nature of a particular space or boundary line.

To demonstrate some of these ambiguous conditions, our slightly tortuous downhill route (Figure 2) from Caine Road to Queen's Road Central (which Google Maps cites as 600 m and a 10-minute walk, if one takes the most direct route along Elgin Street to Bridges Street, and down Shing Wong Street to Gough Street) begins by walking down Elgin Street and turning right, down the stair ramp into the

Figure 3. (top) Vacant lot, Shing Wong Street, surrounded by informal seating (note also the cut logs to the right-hand side of the fence)
Figure 4. (bottom) Boundary line at the Kinwick Center indicated by an inlaid strip of metal edging

Elgin Street Children's Playground. Besides the sign at the entrance, the only other indication of the playground's designated program is a single merry-go-round in the center of the main open space (Figure 5). About 50 sqm, and surrounded on all sides by buildings of over seven stories, the space also contains six benches, one covered table and two fixed chairs, a "foot reflexology" area and a covered drain and a sporadic planting bed around its perimeter. Several large trees shade the space, one of which lost almost a third of its canopy in the 2018 Mangkhut Typhoon. One might be forgiven for assuming this was a park or a Sitting-out Area, if only because its most common use is for sitting, whether by local residents on their lunch break, or by adults reliving their childhood by spinning on the merry-go-round (more often than not, this piece of play equipment is under repair and draped with police tape, which is often ignored) (Figure 5). In the evenings, due to its somewhat hidden location, couples make out or simply hold hands while sitting on the benches, although there is always the risk of mosquito bites – a reason why at certain times of the year no one sits in this not-a-Sitting-out Area. Sometimes people even smoke, an activity strictly forbidden in all government-managed spaces, but if it is late enough at night on a weekend, people are rarely accosted by security. If they are, all they need to do is walk up the back stairs of the open space to the adjacent alley and smoke there, still able to chat with their friends a meter below them (Figure 5). However, despite its name, one does not often see children playing in this space. Given that there is no other play equipment besides the merry-go-round, those who are too young or old for that, or who get bored or too dizzy, repurpose the other equipment in the space for play: the walls, the handrails, the benches and the planters. Playing on these, however is frowned upon by the supervisor of the space, or by local residents who don't want children running around and stepping on their benches, or who are concerned that they could get hurt swinging and jumping on the rails (clearly they are not followers of parkour here). In addition, cycling is not allowed, according to the signs, and this rules out another activity which is barely allowed in Hong Kong. Because of this ambiguity – a playground where only one type of play is sanctioned – the space feels a little desolate. It is used often, just not as it is intended or as well as it could be if it were redesigned with a wider input from the adjacent community and its target user groups – children and parents.

Moving on down the hill through a narrow alley which doubles as a drain in times of heavy rain, another ambiguous, multi-functional space presents itself. The alley serves as the back-of-house for several restaurants, as well as a break, napping, smoking and eating area. This two-meter-wide alley terminates in a decades-old barbershop

Figure 5. Elgin Street Children's Playground — back exit to the adjacent alley and instance
of adult playtime

Figure 6. (previous page) Back alley between Elgin Street Children's Playground and Staunton Street – restaurant back-of-house, hangout, and barbershop

Figure 7. (top) Tsung Wing Lane – back-of-house and front-of-house for bars and restaurants; laundry spaces, AC units, and potted plants

hawker stall and set of stairs before reaching Staunton Street (Figure 6). The walk continues west along this street, turning right after the Mid-Levels Escalator onto Shelley Street.

From here, ambiguous and hybrid conditions appear with increasing frequency and intensity, calling for an inventory to replace a prose description. This approach is adopted to convey just a small portion of the frenetic activity that animates these spaces – 24/7 activities that frustrate a range of desires, either to separate one "type" of open space from another, to create a totalizing topological reading or even to capture these conditions with the single-moment nature of photography:

Turning left onto Tsung Wing Lane before the café Nood and Pure Fitness, both housed in the Kinwick Centre: a steel edge, embedded in the ground defines private and public (Figure 4). Back-of-house mixes with front-of-house/restaurant terraces in the alley right-of-way; servers and cooks smoke while guests in other places eat their pasta; residents hang their laundry amidst AC units and potted plants. Late-night bars with customers sitting and smoking outside are tightly packed into a 0.75 m space on the south side of the alley; a strange, low, fenced-off open space across the way is always entirely vacant – an open space with no use (Figure 7).

Turning right downhill onto Graham Street, then right again into the Graham Street Sitting-out Area: there is play equipment for two- to five-year-olds (which is outdated and rarely used); two wire-mesh benches occupy a two-meter-wide upper level; and a stair connects to a two-meter-wide lower level. This lower level has a concrete checkers-board table, two stools, and two more wire mesh benches. All are covered by canopies that do not protect people from the rain. Lots of mosquitoes accompany a somewhat sparse planting – the area is quite shaded by trees and the adjacent buildings, so it is often moist (dank, even). All in all, the space is quite hidden – an ideal place for sexual activities (one occasionally finds used condoms), for sleeping, and for smoking, as it is rarely used by children (Figure 8). This open space is a dead-end.

Returning to Graham Street and continuing to head downhill, turning left onto Hollywood Road: on the way, passing a popular Instagram spot – a mural of a streetscape of *tung lau* by Alex Croft commissioned by the adjacent Goods of Desire (G.O.D.) homewares shop. Throngs of people mill about in the street and take photos from the opposite sidewalk. There are varying amounts of vehicular traffic on this steep street – but the division between sidewalk and street becomes ambiguous as more tourists jostle for the ideal "beauty spot," inevitably spilling out onto the roadway (Figure 9).

Figure 8. (top) Graham Street Sitting-out Area – mosquitos, checkers, and sex
Figure 9. (bottom) Instagram hot-spot – Alex Croft's mural on the wall of a Goods of Desire
(G.O.D.) shop

Continuing along Hollywood Road, turning right onto Peel Street, then left up an alley stairway into Pak Tze Lane Park. In the alley: smoking, gambling, extensions of restaurants. At night, the park attendant often has to enforce the park's prohibition of smoking, and visitors just step back over the park boundary line (defined only by a change in paving or a trench drain) into the alley to light up. Alcohol is sold 24/7 in Hong Kong, and there is no restriction on open containers, so people regularly spill over into the park from a bar called Club 71, or get drinks from a nearby 7-11, giving the park its colloquial name "Club 7-11" (Figure 10). On the upper terrace of the park, there are some places to sit and a sort of playground, as well as a heritage learning area; the lower terrace has a large sculptural canopy wall which unfolds into tables and seating, but this is not very functional. This area is also patrolled by management (the Leisure and Cultural Services Department, but after a certain hour they are off duty, so the posted park rules (which do not apply to the alleys) are no longer enforced. Located in the center of a block, this park is somewhat hidden, but is often used as a short-cut by those "in the know."

Walking down the Pak Tze Lane stairs through a newly constructed and fancy apartment building underpass (is this now a privately owned public space, or perhaps it always was?), then crossing Gage Street to walk down Staveley Street: there is lots of construction due to the redevelopment of the Gage Street Market area; the lane is an outdoor workshop. It contains restaurant seating, advertising, and almost a feeling of impending doom, with high-end buildings being constructed all around it (Figure 11).

[3] See pp. 270–273 in this volume.

Turning left into Tung Tze Terrace and Wa On Lane Sitting-out Area:[3] a relatively large, multi-level, divided area. There is a mish-mash of different types of open space; a mix of free-standing and built-in benches, most of which are rarely used except for the ones covered by a canopy; a circular rubber ground surface that has a single, four-toddler, plastic teeter-totter on a spring; and a "Fitness Corner for the Elderly," all on the middle level of the open space. On the upper level, there is a covered toddler slide on a square of rubber surface, with a tic-tac-toe wall, and a slatted wooden table and fixed chairs opposite it. A privately owned public walkway comprises the west entrance to the space from Aberdeen Street and the back door of the Mingle (hourly) Hotel exits into the park from the north. This space was once quite dark and shady, but with the loss of trees in the 2018 Typhoon Mangkhut, the fairly lush under-planting is thriving and the space now feels more open and inviting.

Figure 10. Looking east at Pak Tze Lane Park (left side of the photo) and alley (right side of the photo)

The tour ends here, having passed through two children's playgrounds, a park, a Sitting-out Area, a seemingly vacant lo and several alleys, stairs and streets. What all of these interstitial or hybrid spaces have in common is the evidence they provide of unseen conditions, unwritten codes or self-generating cultural and social forces. They respond to adjacencies or environmental conditions. Their actual use and occupation often directly ignores or subverts the posted (or unposted) rules and frequently does not conform to the generally happenstance, formal nomenclature. In other words, when these interstitial sites are also considered as places for people, in addition to being categorized according to who owns or manages them, or according to the desired program (as they are by the city), or analyzed according to their geographical, topographical, ecological or historical origins and settings (as they are in this volume), we can begin to see that they afford specific niches for a variety of everyday, and often quite particularized, behaviors, installations, adaptations, formal plantings, spontaneous plant life, noise, sunlight and shade conditions, and all manner of other social, ecological and material life. With this in mind, we can now begin to recognize the very specific temporal and socio-cultural conditions within and surrounding these spaces themselves, to which the utilization of these spaces actually respond – conditions that have very little to do with their formal designations. This everyday appropriation is a common thematic, which can be applied not only to the way that these spaces are classified in the nomenclature of the authors, but also to the way that people themselves use these spaces. These uses are sometimes an unknowing response to the codes that regulate the spaces; or a direct response to the adjacencies; or, at other times, based on a case-by-case, hour-by-hour individual judgment of what should be the normative and normalized behavior in these in-between spaces.

Although the very existence, as well as the formal and spatial qualities, of the Sitting-out Areas and Rest Gardens are often determined by accidental openings in the building fabric, which then adapt to their site, the behavior of those who use these open spaces has very little to do with their formal typology. Instead, that behavior has everything to do with what users can get away with in one space versus another. To the visitor, it is often difficult to distinguish, and even less important to care, whether an open space is a Sitting-out Area, a children's playground, a park or a sidewalk. Although the subject of this book is the spaces known as "Sitting-out Areas" and "Rest Gardens," this nomenclature often does little to actually indicate the potential uses of the spaces, and vice versa. This naming is primarily related to who developed, designed and/or manages them. Such naming also effects a kind of normative flattening, implying a homogeneity across these spaces that does not exist in reality.

Figure 11: Looking south up Stanley Street – gentrifying alleys in the Gage Street Market area; hipsters are literally displacing dai pai dong

Note: In her introduction to the book *London: Aspects of Change* in 1964, the urban sociologist Ruth Glass coined the term "gentrification," which refers to the arrival of middle and upper-middle class people in an existing urban district, a related increase in rents and property values and changes in the district's character and culture.

Conclusion

There are two complementary tendencies at work in these spaces which frustrate a topological reading:

1. The porosity of the spaces and the uncertainty of their boundaries and thresholds leads to ambiguities in their taxonomical status and usage. If the physical definition of the space is not clear, this opens up the possibility for a slipperiness in the definition of acceptable uses.

2. It is exactly the habitual appropriation of spaces for whatever use might be required or necessary in the space – no matter what the formal definition or classification or designated rules – that creates conditions where their boundaries and thresholds seem ambiguous and uncertain.

These conditions are part of what defines the compelling character of urban spaces in Hong Kong and should be recognized as a distinctive kind of urban heritage or cultural landscape. They lay the foundation for the micro-urbanism of Hong Kong's streets, alleyways, stairs, Sitting-out Areas, playgrounds, parks, vacant plots, leftover spaces and innumerable other pockets and glitches where the urban fabric does not quite align or resolve into clearly defined parcels and usages. What Benjamin and Lacis said of Naples so many years ago remains true of Hong Kong today: "no figure asserts it's 'thus and not otherwise'" (1978). In fact, the reverse is probably even more true for Hong Kong's ambiguous topologies of public open space – never thus, and always otherwise.

References

Benjamin, Walter and Asja Lacis. 1978. Naples. *Walter Benjamin, Reflections: Essays, Aphorisms, Autobiographical Writings*. Trans. Peter Demetz, ed. Edmund Jephcott, Harcourt Brace Jovanovich. New York: Harcourt Brace Jovanovich. 163–173.

Borio, Géraldine and Caroline Wüthrich. 2015. *Hong Kong In-Between*. Hong Kong and Zurich: MCCM Creations and Park Books.

Cheung, Esther. 2003. Voices of negotiation in late twentieth-century Hong Kong literature. *The Columbia Companion to Modern East Asian Literature*. Joshua Mostow, Kirk Denton, Bruce Fulton and Sharalyn Orbaugh. New York: Columbia University Press. 604–609.

Fraser, Alistair and Eva Cheuk-Yin Li. 2017. The second life of Kowloon Walled City: Crime, media and cultural memory. *Crime Media Culture* 13 (2): 217–234.

Girot, Christophe. 2013. The Elegance of Topology. *Topology*. Ed. Christophe Girot, Anette Freytag, Albert Kirchengast and Dunja Richter. Landscript 3. Berlin: jovis.

Kai-Cheung, Dung. 2012. *Atlas: The Archaeology of an Imaginary City*. Trans. Dung Kai-cheung, Anders Hansson, and Bonnie S. McDougall. New York: Columbia University Press. (Originally published as *Dituji – yi ge xiangxiang de chengshi de kaoguxue*. 1997. Taipei, Unitas Publishing Co.).

Leung, Ping-kwan. 1998. The Walled City in Kowloon: A space we all shared. In *Hong Kong Collage: Contemporary Stories and Writing*. ed. Martha P.Y. Cheung. Hong Kong: Oxford University Press. 34–39.

Lynn, Greg. 1993. Folding in architecture. *Architectural Design* 63 (March–April): 8–15.

OED Online. topology, noun. December 2018. Oxford University Press. http://www.oed.com/view/Entry/203426?redirectedFrom=topology (Accessed January 13, 2019). See definitions 1 and 2.

Taylor, Jeremy E. 2003. Nation, topography, and historiography: Writing topographical histories in Hong Kong. *Modern Chinese Literature and Culture*, 14 (2): 45–74.

Tuan, Yi-Fu. 1974. *Topophilia: A Study of Environmental Perception, Attitudes, and Values*. Englewood Cliffs, NJ: Prentice-Hall.

Reassembling the Case Study:
Critical Analysis and Design Production in the Studio

Ivan Valin

In Studio

The research compiled in this book was initiated as part of a teaching exercise developed by the authors for an introductory design studio in the in the Master of Landscape Architecture program at the University of Hong Kong (Figure 1). As fundamental subjects in any landscape design education, issues of typology and of small-scale site design strategy had been addressed in earlier iterations of the course. Hong Kong is celebrated as an outdoor laboratory for students in the disciplines of urban design, architecture and occasionally, landscape architecture. Often described as a three-dimensional city, famed for its conditions of extreme density, world-class transportation, pencil towers and town-sized estates, there are countless cases of architectural, engineering and planning achievements to study, emulate and improve upon. Our teaching and research seeks value in those parts of this outdoor laboratory in areas that have been generally invisible or unnoticed. By introducing a rigorous, multi-year case study exercise focused on the small and undervalued urban open space fragments presented in this book, the authors have also developed a pedagogy that understands the city from its exceptions, and that approaches the case study method as an open, generative technique.

The design studio sits at the heart of most environmental design discipline curricula and has developed around a unique set of pedagogical norms and teaching practices (Crowther 2013; Dutton 1987; Schön 1984). Design studio problems may be drawn from real-world situations or woven out of abstracted conditions in response to disciplinary theories and methodologies. While architecture, urban planning, urban design and landscape architecture design studio approaches have their own disciplinary goals, all utilize a recognizable set of learning activities that are problem-based, experiential, active, critical and iterative (Kuhn 2001; Long 2012; Steinitz 1990). Studio courses are structured to teach students to synthesize project information with their own analytical work, to develop rational but creative responses to complex problems and

Figure 1. Students, instructors, and guests discussing a design and research project in a
public exhibition and review

to work iteratively and self-critically under the expectations and limitations of project delivery. The organization, spaces, form and even language of studio design education is often traced back to the Beaux-Arts tradition. Despite frequent attempts at reform, the design studio survives in a form that is recognizable today from its nineteenth-century origins. But the studio pedagogy is not monolithic, and recent teaching practices have closely tracked shifts in theory, technology and the changing realities of professional practice. The contemporary design studio has been harnessed to produce original research (Armstrong 1999; Varnelis 2007); to experiment with disciplinary methods intended to inform professional practice (Yang & Li 2016); or to perform quasi-professional services or community-based design (Forsyth, Lu & McGirr 1999).

The Case Study Method in Design Education

The case study method is a fundamental part of design studio instruction and is often situated as part of an "information-gathering" research exercise that prefaces the student's own response to a design problem (Salama 2016). A carefully chosen case study provides an example of how a similar set of issues or standards were resolved and, through a comparison across multiple case-studies, how differences in context and problem resolve in different design outcomes. In the architecture and landscape architecture disciplines, the case study method looked traditionally only at historically important works that had been collectively defined to typify a desired set of disciplinary principles and thus learning outcomes. Beginning in the 1970s however, the problems of the city and society began to impact the environmental design fields, particularly in the fields of urban planning and landscape architecture. In response, design education in these fields began to concern itself with the urban experience and case studies shifted away from appreciating the internal rigor of canonical monument objects and towards the strategies underlying the organic complexities of the urban fabric: the lived-in street, formal and informal community structures, transportation systems and open space networks. Anne Vernez-Moudon described the emergence of "typomorphological studies" as eschewing the aesthetic-based analysis of objects for a more open-ended assessment of the spaces and structures of a city – in time and through negotiation, within a socio-political environment (1994).

In his 2001 piece for *Landscape Journal*, Mark Francis examines the emergence of case studies specifically within the landscape architecture discipline in an effort to codify their methodologies within education, research and practice (2001). Francis distinguishes between case studies that are descriptive of a project or process, and those that illuminate the theories and practices underlying a specific outcome. The lack of a systematic approach to gathering and analyzing data on a given project, he argues, is at odds with this synthetic approach. Though Francis argues in favor of large and standardized "archives" of valuable case study projects for the discipline's collective use, he also notes that contemporary practice recognizes the problems of transferability arising from such databases. Effective case studies, in as much as they attempt to go beyond physical and material descriptions, should be sensitive to the underlying social, economic, ecological, political and technological milieus of the place and time in question.

(Inter)positioning: Transformations in City and Terrain

The teaching exercise described below draws on the tradition of case study analysis on the unique open space typology of the Sitting-out Area. The five-and-a-half week project was structured into two parts: the first, an analysis; the second, a translation. Rather than presenting the case study as a stand-alone work from which lessons are derived, here the case study research output is re-processed and re-contextualized through an abbreviated design process resulting in an original work. The aim of this methodology is to develop the students' analytical skills while also promoting their spatial literacy and a typomorpohological appreciation for the urban landscapes of Hong Kong. A larger goal for the exercise, as for the introductory studio itself, was to initiate a critical discourse on the underlying values and conflicts over ownership, ecology, space and technology that are represented in the public realm of a high-density Asian metropolis.

Sitting-out Areas and Rest Gardens were chosen as both the subject of the case study and the physical site for the design exercise. As this book attests, these small public spaces are the consequence of a unique set of underlying conditions and territorial histories; they are valued by many local communities as a key open space amenity and a crucial component of a larger public realm network; yet municipal planners have failed to capitalize on these strengths to realize larger social and ecological benefits. Important but overlooked, we recognized these small spaces as a perfect subject for academic exploration. In this regard, our project and approach is indebted to scholars and educators who have – through their teaching and research – described the value of the everyday, ordinary or unseen components of the urban fabric. Margaret Crawford, William Whyte,

GRAHAM STREET
SITTING OUT AREA
URBAN POCKET MONUMENTS

ADDRESS: 54 Graham Street
SIZE: 133.2 SQM
NO. OF SEATS: 15

The Graham Street Sitting Out Area is built in a densely developed neighbourhood of SOHO. The sitting out area built in a empty tonglau space and is surrounded by residential blocks with narrow opening to the road. Due to the urban development towards PaiPingShan, the urban space was designed to cope with the sloped ground and the sitting out area is following the urban grid with leveled landscape.

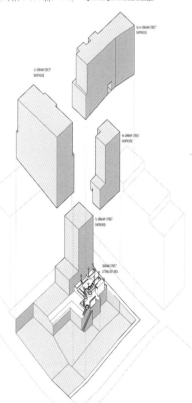

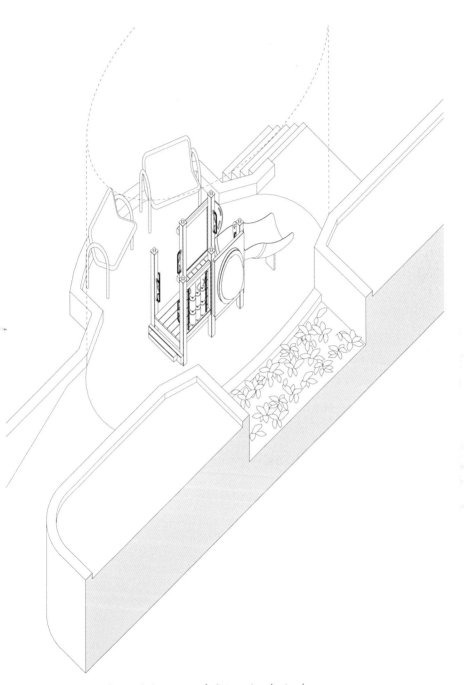

Figure 2. (previous page) Initial case study documentation of a Sitting-out Area showing plan detail, site usage and urban context. Work by Sushakri Chow, 2016

Figure 3. (top) An observed spatial assembly composed of two seats facing a level patch of paving, play-equipment and shaped planters. Work by Sushakri Chow, 2016

Clare Cooper Marcus, contemporary design scholars including Jonathan Solomon et al. and the works of Atelier Bow-Wow each developed, through their mundane case studies, a set of repeatable analytical methods contributing to their own theories of urbanism and describing a set of strategies for design (Chase, Crawford & Kaliski 1999; Frampton, Solomon & Wong 2012; Kuroda, Kaijima & Tsukamoto 2001). Small and common are also very practical traits for structuring a learning exercise that demands field work. Many different sites were available to busy students, each of an ideal size to allow a careful documentation within a short period of time. This stands in contrast to many contemporary approaches to teaching landscape architecture that increasingly deal with research and field work at the scale of landscape systems or entire territories. With more than 500 possible Sitting-out Areas and Rest Gardens to choose from in Hong Kong, we focused on a different set of districts in each of the three years that this course was taught. Students within each of the three cohorts of 36 students were assigned sites randomly within these areas. In 2016, the students surveyed sites within Hong Kong's Central, Western, and Wan Chai Districts; in 2017, sites were located in Kowloon District; and finally in 2018, the sites allocated were in the Eastern and Southern Districts.

The Survey

The first part of this teaching exercise, called the Illustrated Survey, comprised field work, spatial abstraction and purposeful representation. Students visited their prescribed Sitting-out Area or Rest Garden site to document its physical dimensions; observe its users; and note the surrounding built, topographical and ecological context. Working individually, students used photographs and sketches to capture the essential details and character of each site. Information that would normally be available as public data in other cities, on locations, boundaries or amenities, is not available in Hong Kong's public land databases. In fact, the most complete source of Sitting-out Areas data compiled and maintained by Government was, at the time of this research, simply a list of public spaces designated as "smoking areas." Due to the lack of any detailed or organized data available to the public, the survey was an important step in verifying existing information and generating new data. Sites and their contexts were discussed in class as provisional and subject to change – a standard truism in landscape architectural thinking, but especially true for these small and undervalued spaces. Some Sitting-out Areas are quietly subsumed in the face of Hong Kong's rapidly changing urban fabric. Others are designated with signage as "temporary" amenities, blatantly waiting for a better land utilization.

Figure 4. Plan/elevation composite drawing of a redesigned Sitting-out Area. Work by
Zhengzheng Xiong, 2017

The products of the Illustrated Survey included a brief interpretation of the underlying organization of the site, a plan and section drawn from site measurements and an analysis of the urban and ecological context (Figure 2). Additionally, students were required to select two enlarged areas for a more detailed focus. Termed the "spatial assemblage," these focal areas were chosen based on the reading of the site as a sequence of spaces with differing amounts of programmatic and circulatory specificity. The spatial assemblages tended to be areas of intersection, enclosure, transition, layering or any other intentional spatial configuration. Once these were selected, students were required to redraw an axonometric projection of the assemblage as a discrete object isolated from its surroundings (Figure 3).

The concept of the spatial assemblage was derived from our own observations about the Sitting-out Area and Rest Garden as the most ambiguous class of public realm in the city. These small open spaces are ostensibly intended to provide a site for passive recreation at a local level. But pre-existing, difficult conditions combined with an off-the-shelf approach to implementation have produced a near endless set of spatial configurations. These discrete and describable arrangements of furniture, structure, paving and plants allow instructors to lead clear discussions about design as it is resolved in form, scale, program and detail – learning outcomes that are common in case-study exercises. But in contrast to these traditional learning outcomes, the conversations around design in this exercise were expected to be inquisitive. We asked the students to work like anthropologists instead of design critics by focusing on contextualizing the case study, as a whole and in detail, through a particular set of codes and practices and within a particular socio-political, environmental reality. The spatial assemblages, as points of intersection of all of these forces range from the obvious to the bizarre, capturing sublime moments of juxtaposition or revealing the absurdities of the planning process. The isolated fragment became a way for students to interrogate the spaces and relationships found in existing Sitting-out Areas and to visualize the lost opportunities therein. The diverse catalog of spaces collected by each cohort ultimately provided a lens through which to discuss the mechanisms of high-density urbanization and the specific challenges of building within Hong Kong's terrain.

The Transformation

The second part of this teaching exercise, called Type Transformations, asked students to redesign their case study site in a way that improved its social or environmental performance. The critical contextual observations developed in the first part of the exercise became the design brief for this second phase of transformation. In articulating their design transformation, students were limited to utilizing only the spatial assemblies drawn from other students' case studies (Figure 5). This aspect of the project was an interpretation of a method of blind collaboration along the lines of the cadavre exquis deployed more commonly in the visual arts. We found this method equally suggestive of the forced inefficiencies and arbitrary constraints that are found in actual design practice for public projects in Hong Kong. Less cynically, our aim in this part of the exercise was to remove form-making from the student's initial design process and to avoid more advanced design consideration of structural limitations or material selection.

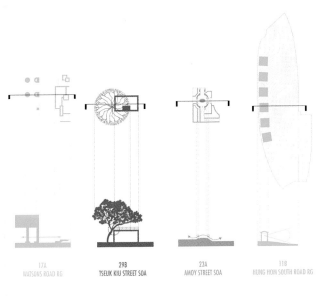

17A	29B	23A	11B
WATSONS ROAD RG	TSEUK KIU STREET SOA	AMOY STREET SOA	HUNG HOM SOUTH ROAD RG

Figure 5. A selection of spatial assemblies, extracted from their respective Sitting-out Areas. Work by Shing Chun Chu, 2018

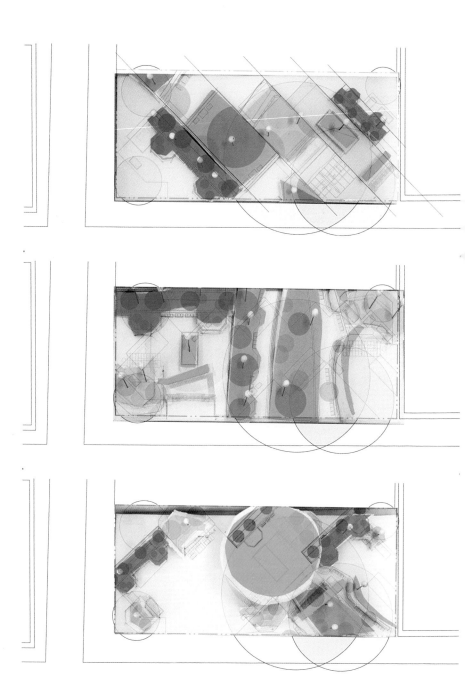

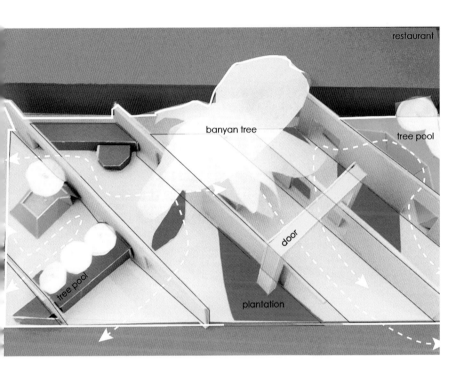

restaurant

banyan tree

tree pool

door

tree pool

plantation

Figure 6. (previous page) Three-dimensional collage tests with color-coded spatial assemblies borrowed from other sites. Work by Fan Lu, 2017

Figure 7. (top) Students are also expected to develop their spatial collage through physical models to create new programs and site relationships. Work by Fan Lu, 2017

Students were introduced to the concept of collage and its deep history in the design and art disciplines. Collage had emerged as a popular graphic technique in landscape architecture in the mid-1990s — with the work of landscape architects like James Corner and Adriaan Geuze. They in turn drew on a range of precedents including work by the architects Rem Koolhaas and Mies van der Rohe, and by artists from Hannah Höch to David Hockney. Our pedagogical aims for this part of the exercise drew more on the theoretical aspects of collage as initially developed by Picasso, in which the montage techniques allowed the simultaneity of varied realities in a unified space. New meaning was generated through juxtaposition and unexpected associations (Rekittke & Paar 2008). From the initial process of pastiche, the collage methodology allowed students to transform their appropriated spatial assemblies through simple modifications like scaling, distorting, clipping and repetition in order to generate design outcomes that suited the existing conditions of their site (Figures 6, 7). Color-coded models and drawings revealed the origins of each material fragment and allowed, through successive iterations of models and drawings, the process of transformation and tuning to be tracked and discussed. Successful student projects brought together their borrowed spatial assemblies in ways that generated new spaces in their overlap or adjacencies (Figure 8).

Results

At the conclusion of the exercise, students presented a proposal for a new Sitting-out Area on the site of their original case study (Figure 4, 9). These 36 imaginary Sitting-out Areas that were produced each year sit alongside 36 carefully documented Sitting-out Area case studies, like fun-house mirrors held up to a unique spatial phenomenon in the city. More than simple creative alternatives, the proposals stand as critical reconfigurations of the corpus of responses to unseen, unquestioned codes and restrictions relating to the construction of the public realm in the city. The shorthand typological categories presented in this book – Rift, Misfit, Gap, Littoral, Lacuna, Lapse – guided a student-led discussion about the design of the public realm in the city around issues of geology, infrastructure, density, ecology, history and edge.

A multi-year studio format has allowed us to build institutional knowledge through successive waves of student research and studio experiences as we canvased the numerous Sitting-out Areas and Rest Gardens in the city. Student-derived information and insight is all the more important in engaging with the urban landscape, especially where official resources are underdeveloped. Our categorical

Figure 8. Students create new spatial assemblies for their design proposals, revealing links to material and structural precedent from their case studies. Work by Zhengzheng Xiong, 2017 (left); Chun Yin Yuen, 2018 (right)

definitions, our understanding of the spatial and material scope of the Sitting-out Area and our appreciation for novel solutions within fixed means was informed by the student-led research and input. By working through successive iterations of teaching within a clearly framed overall research interest, we were able to ask each new cohort of design students to critically evaluate and expand upon previous efforts in depth and breadth. Each year's group was able to refine and build upon the work of the previous group. To facilitate this knowledge transfer, we opted to perform intermediate and final project reviews in a "public gallery" style, inviting other students to participate in the critique and examine the work (Figure 10).

The case study method that deals in the ordinary components of the city – in our case, the sometimes extra-ordinary open space typologies of the Sitting-out Areas and Rest Gardens – positions the design student as inspector and interpreter. Instructor and student examine each case study together, helping to break down the mentor-disciple relationship between instructor and students that typically prevails in the design studio. The resulting teaching relationship is student-led. To augment the active learning aspects of a student-lead process, we did not hold predetermined lesson goals from the case study method beyond those related to a clear and concise documentation and spatial description. Hong Kong's Sitting-out Areas and Rest Gardens are in no way model design solutions, and often quite the opposite. Since they are not canonical works of excellence, they do not represent embodied expertise. Rather, students in their own investigations are responsible for evaluating their cases as a set of responses to existing conditions. Because each student works on a different case study and different site, knowledge within the studio is developed primarily through latitudinal comparisons. One student's research is reinterpreted through another student's design translation. Thus, the students are positioned to learn from those things they identify as successful, while refining their abilities as design critics in explaining those things that fail. Both student and instructor are involved in a conversation of critical interpretation and evaluation. Ultimately, the teaching experience, explored alongside the research initiative presented in this book, engages the city as a laboratory and argues for a design pedagogy that links active learning to a focused appraisal of the city. Landscape design pedagogy is pursued as a form of cultural and environmental engagement, while teaching methods that are student-led, active, iterative and self-critical are set as a counterpoint to passive or overly prescriptive, outcome-driven techniques to design instruction that prevail today.

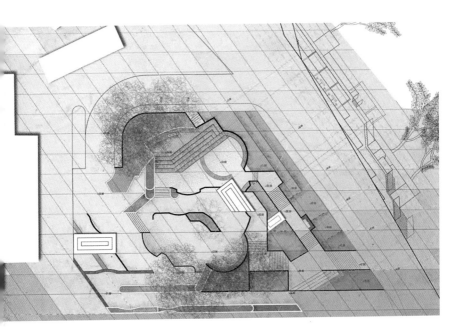

Figure 9. The final Sitting-out Area site design after iterative development. Work by Hiu Yan Wong, 2016 (top); Shing Chun Chu, 2018 (bottom)

Figure 10. Gallery style public reviews give students an opportunity to share their work and process with invited guests and other students

References

Armstrong, H. 1999. Design studios as research: An emerging paradigm for landscape architecture. *Landscape Review* 5 (2): 5–25.

Chase, J., M. Crawford and J. Kaliski. 1999. *Everyday Urbanism: Featuring John Chase*. New York, N.Y.: Monacelli Press.

Crowther, P. 2013. Understanding the signature pedagogy of the design studio and the opportunities for its technological enhancement. Special issue, *Journal of Learning Design* Vol 6.

Dutton, T. A. 1987. Design and Studio Pedagogy. *Journal of Architectural Education* 41 (1): 16–25.

Forsyth, A., H. Lu and P. McGirr. 1999. Inside the service learning studio in urban design. *Landscape Journal* 18 (2): 166–178.

Frampton, A., J. Solomon and C. Wong. 2012. *Cities Without Ground: A Hong Kong Guidebook*. New York: Oro Editions.

Kuhn, S. 2001. Learning from the architecture studio: Implications for project-based pedagogy. *International Journal of Engineering Education* 17 (4/5): 349–352.

Kuroda, J., M. Kaijima and Y. Tsukamoto. 2001. *Made in Tokyo*. Tokyo, Japan: Kajima Institute Publishing Co.

Long, J. G. 2012. State of the studio. *Journal of Planning Education and Research* 32 (4): 431–448.

Moudon, A. V. 1994. Getting to know the built landscape: typomorphology. In *Ordering Space: Types in Architecture and Design,* ed. K. A. Franck & L. H. Schneekloth, New York: Van Nostrand Reinhold. 289–311.

Rekittke, J., and D. P. Paar. 2008. Real-time collage in landscape architecture. In *Digital Design in Landscape Architecture*, ed. E. Buhmann, M. Pietsch & M. Heins, Heidelberg, Wichmann. 88–95.

Salama, A. M. 2015. *Spatial Design Education: New Directions for Pedagogy in Architecture and Beyond*. Surrey, England: Ashgate.

Schön, D. A. 1984. The architectural studio as an exemplar of education for reflection-in-action. *Journal of Architectural Education,* 38 (1): 2–9.

Steinitz, C. 1990. A framework for theory applicable to the education of landscape architects (and other environmental design professionals). *Landscape Journal* 9 (2): 136–143.

Varnelis, K. 2007. Is there research in the studio?. *Journal of Architectural Education* 61 (1): 11–14.

Yang, B., and S. Li. 2016. Design with nature: Ian McHarg's ecological wisdom as actionable and practical knowledge. *Landscape and Urban Planning* 155: 21–32.

PART 2:
Cases

Short-lived, rough in detail, unremarkable in design – the Sitting-out Areas and Rest Gardens found throughout Hong Kong fill an essential niche, providing a miniature moment of rest against the unrelenting fabric of the dense city.

Central & Western

| 1 | Belcher's Street Sitting-out Area | 2 | Bonham Road Rest Garden | 3 | Caine Road Sitting-out Area | 4 | Centre Street Sitting-out Area | 5 | Chater Road Sitting-out Area | 6 | Chung Wo Lane Sitting-out Area | 7 | Cleverly Street Sitting-out Area | 8 | Cochrane Street Sitting-out Area | **9 | Conduit Road Rest Garden** | 10 | Fung Mat Road Sitting-out Area | 11 | Graham Street Sitting-out Area | 12 | Guildford Road Rest Garden | 13 | Hatton Road Sitting-out Area | 14 | Hill Road Rest Garden | 15 | Ka Wai Man Road Sitting-out Area | 16 | Kennedy Town Bus Terminus Sitting-out Area | **17 | Kotewall Road Rest Garden** | 18 | Kotewall Road Sitting-out Area | 19 | Lambeth Walk Rest Garden | 20 | Lan Kwai Fong Sitting-out Area | 21 | Lok Hing Lane Temporary Sitting-out Area | 22 | Lower Albert Road Sitting-out Area | 23 | Mount Austin Road Rest Garden | 24 | Mount Davis Service Reservoir Sitting-out Area | 25 | Mount Davis Sitting-out Area No.1 | 26 | Mount Davis Sitting-out Area No.2 | 27 | Mount Davis Sitting-out Area No.3 | 28 | Mount Davis Temporary Sitting-out Area | 29 | Mui Fong Street Sitting-out Area | 30 | Oaklands Avenue Sitting-out Area | 31 | Old Peak Road Rest Garden | **32 | Peel Rise Rest Garden** | 33 | Pier Road Sitting-out Area | 34 | Pok Fu Lam Road Sitting-out Area | **35 | Pokfield Road Sitting-out Area** | 36 | Queen Street Rest Garden | 37 | Robinson Road/ Seymour Road Sitting-out Area | 38 | Robinson Road Sitting-out Area | 39 | Rock Hill Street Sitting-out Area | **40 | Sai On Lane Rest Garden** | 41 | Sai Yuen Lane Sitting-out Area | 42 | Sheung Fung Lane Sitting-out Area | 43 | Sitting-out Area under Flyover in Bonham Road | **44 | Sitting-out Area under Flyover in Hill Road** | 45 | Sitting-out Area under Flyover in Pok Fu Lam Road | 46 | Third Street Sitting-out Area | 47 | Upper Station Street Sitting-out Area | **48 | Wa On Lane Sitting-out Area | 49 | Wing Lee Street Rest Garden** | 50 | Wing Lee Street Sitting-out Area

Wan Chai

| 51 | Amoy Street Sitting-out Area | 52 | Blue Pool Road Sitting-out Area | 53 | Bowen Road Temporary Sitting-out Area | 54 | Broadwood Road Rest Garden | 55 | Bullock Lane Sitting-out Area | 56 | Dragon Road Sitting-out Area | **57 | Eastern Hospital Road Sitting-out Area** | 58 | Eastern Hospital Road Temporary Rest Garden | 59 | Electric Road Sitting-out Area | 60 | Gloucester Road/Cannon Street Sitting-out Area | 61 | Green Lane Service Reservoir Sitting-out Area | 62 | Hennessy Road/Johnston Road Sitting-out Area | **63 | Kennedy Street Sitting-out Area** | 64 | Lau Sin Street Temporary Sitting-out Area | 65 | Lin Fa Kung Street East Sitting-out Area | 66 | Lun Fat Street Sitting-out Area | 67 | Lun Fat Street Rest Garden | 68 | Monmouth Terrace Sitting-out Area | 69 | Mount Butler Sitting-out Area | 70 | Perkin's Road Sitting-out Area | 71 | Queen's Road East/Hennessy Road Sitting-out Area | 72 | Queen's Road East/ Swatow Street Sitting-out Area | 73 | Sing Woo Road Rest Garden | 74 | Spring Garden Lane Sitting-out Area | 75 | Stubbs Road Sitting-out Area | 76 | Tai Hang Drive Sitting-out Area | 77 | Tai Hang Road Rest Garden | 78 | Tai Tam Reservoir Road Sitting-out Area | 79 | Tai Wong Street East Sitting-out Area | 80 | Tung Lo Wan Road Sitting-out Area | 81 | Tunnel Approach Rest Garden | 82 | Wan Chai Gap Road Sitting-out Area | 83 | Watson Road Rest Garden | **84 | Whitfield Road Rest Garden** | 85 | Wing Ning Street Sitting-out Area | 86 | Wong Nai Chung Gap Sitting-out Area | 87 | Wong Nai Chung Road Rest Garden | 88 | Wong Nai Chung Road Sitting-out Area

Eastern

| 89 | Braemar Hill Road Sitting-out Area | 90 | Chai Wan Road Sitting-out Area No. 1 | 91 | Chai Wan Road Sitting-out Area No. 2 | **92 | Chai Wan Road Temporary Rest Garden** | 93 | Cheung Man Road Rest Garden | 94 | Ching Wah Street Sitting-out Area | 95 | Church Street Sitting-out Area | **96 | Comfort Terrace Rest Garden** | 97 | Fei Tsui Road Sitting-out Area | 98 | Finnie Street Sitting-out Area | 99 | Fu Hong Street Sitting-out Area | 100 | Greig Road Sitting-out Area | 101 | Hoi Ning Street Sitting-out Area | 102 | Hong Cheung Street Sitting-out Area | 103 | Kam Wah Street Rest Garden | **104 | Law Uk Folk Museum Rest Garden** | 105 | Lei King Wan Sitting-out Area | 106 | Lok Man Road Sitting-out Area | 107 | Miu Tung Street Sitting-out Area | 108 | Mong Lung Street Sitting-out Area | 109 | Mount Park Road Sitting-out Area | 110 | Nam On Street Sitting-out Area | 111 | Nam On Street/Sun Shing Street Sitting-out Area | 112 | Ngoi Man Street Sitting-out Area | 113 | North Point Salt Water Service Reservoir Sitting-out Area | 114 | Quarry Bay Wilson Trail Sitting-out Area | **115 | San Ha Street Sitting-out Area** | 116 | Shau Kei Wan Market Building Sitting-out Area | 117 | Shau Kei Wan Road Sitting-out Area | 118 | Tai Lok Street Sitting-out Area | 119 | Tai Man Street Sitting-out Area | 120 | Tin Hau Temple Road Sitting-out Area | 121 | Wharf Road Rest Garden | 122 | Yee Shing Lane Temporary Sitting-out Area | 123 | Yee Tai Street Sitting-out Area | 124 | Yiu Hing Street Sitting-out Area

Southern

| 125 | Aberdeen Boulder's Corner Rest Garden | 126 | Aberdeen Praya Road Sitting-out Area | 127 | Aberdeen Reservoir Road Sitting-out Area | 128 | Ap Lei Chau Main Street Temporary Sitting-out Area | **129 | Heung Yip Road Sitting-out Area No. 2** | 130 | Hung Shing Street Rest Garden | 131 | Kwun Hoi Path Sitting-out Area | 132 | Lee Nam Road Sitting-out Area No. 1 | 133 | Lee Nam Road Sitting-out Area No. 2 | 134 | Nam Fung Road Rest Garden | 135 | Nam Long Shan Road Children's Playground and Rest Garden | 136 | Nam Long Shan Road Rest Garden | 137 | Nam Long Shan Road Sitting-out Area | 138 | Nam Ning Street Sitting-out Area | **139 | Old Main Street Rest Garden** | 140 | Pok Fu Lam Village Sitting-out Area No.1 | 141 | Pok Fu Lam Village Sitting-out Area No.2 | 142 | San Shi Street Sitting-out Area | **143 | Sassoon Road Rest Garden** | 144 | Shek O Beach Sitting-out Area | 145 | Shek O Village Sitting-out Area | 146 | Shum Wan Road Sitting-out Area | **147 | Sitting-out Area at Aberdeen Main Road/Ap Lei Chau Bridge Flyover** | 148 | South Bay Road Rest Garden | 149 | Southern District San Wai Village Sitting-out Area | 150 | Stanley Beach Road Sitting-out Area | 151 | Stanley Link Road Sitting-out Area | 152 | Stanley Market Road Sitting-out Area | 153 | Stanley New Street/Stanley Village Road Sitting-out Area | **154 | Sun Pat Kan Sitting-out Area** | 155 | Upper Kai Lun Wan Temporary Sitting-out Area | 156 | Wah Chui Street Sitting-out Area | **157 | Wah Lam Path Sitting-out Area** | 158 | Wong Chuk Hang Service Reservoir Rest Garden | 159 | Wong Ma Kok Road Temporary Sitting-out Area | 160 | Yip Kan Street Sitting-out Area | **161 | Yuk Kwai Shan Service Reservoir Sitting-out Area**

Sham Shui Po

| 162 | Berwick Street Sitting-out Area | 163 | Castle Peak Road Sitting-out Area | 164 | Castle Peak Road/Ching Cheung Road Rest Garden | 165 | Cheung Sha Wan Path Sitting-out Area | 166 | Fuk Wah Street Rest Garden | 167 | Fuk Wing Street Rest Garden | 168 | Lei Cheng Uk Swimming Pool Rest Garden | 169 | Lei Cheng Uk Swimming Pool Sitting-out Area No.2 | 170 | Magnolia Road Rest Garden | 171 | Nam Cheong Street Rest Garden | 172 | Nam Cheong Street Sitting-out Area | 173 | Nam Cheong Street/Tai Po Road Rest Garden | 174 | Osmanthus Road Rest Garden | 175 | Shek Kip Mei Street Rest Garden | 176 | Tai Hang Sai Street Sitting-out Area | 177 | Tai Hang Tung Sitting-out Area | 178 | Tai Po Road/Castle Peak Road Rest Garden | 179 | Tseuk Kiu Street Sitting-out Area | 180 | Wai Chi Street Rest Garden | 181 | Wing Hong Street Rest Garden

Yau Tsim Mong

| 182 | Arran Street Sitting-out Area | 183 | Austin Road Sitting-out Area | 184 | Beech Street Sitting-out Area | 185 | Canton Road/Dundas Street Sitting-out Area | 186 | Canton Road/Nelson Street Sitting-out Area | 187 | Canton Road/Soy Street Sitting-out Area | 188 | Cherry Street Sitting-out Area | 189 | Changsha Street Sitting-out Area | 190 | Chui Yu Road Rest Garden | 191 | Dundas Street Sitting-out Area | 192 | Gascoigne Road/Nathan Road Rest Garden (Stage I) | 193 | Hamilton Street Rest Garden | 194 | Ivy Street Rest Garden | 195 | King's Park Rest Garden | **196 | Kowloon Park Drive Rest Garden** | 197 | Lai Chi Kok Road/Tai Nam Street Sitting-out Area | 198 | Luen Wan Street Sitting-out Area | 199 | Man Cheong Street Rest Garden | 200 | Man Ming Lane Rest Garden | 201 | Nathan Road/Boundary Street Sitting-out Area | 202 | Ning Po Street/Shanghai Street Rest Garden | 203 | Nullah Road Sitting-out Area | 204 | Peking Road Sitting-out Area | **205 | Portland Street Rest Garden** | 206 | Portland Street Sitting-out Area | 207 | Portland Street/Man Ming Lane Sitting-out Area | 208 | Public Square Street Rest Garden | 209 | Public Square Street Sitting-out Area | 210 | Public Square Street/Cliff Road Sitting-out Area | 211 | Public Square Street/Kansu Street Rest Garden | 212 | Reclamation Street Sitting-out Area | 213 | Reclamation Street/Nelson Street Sitting-out Area | 214 | Reclamation Street/Soy Street Sitting-out Area | 215 | Shanghai Street/Dundas Street Sitting-out Area | 216 | Shanghai Street/Shantung Street Sitting-out Area | 217 | Shan Tung Street Sitting-out Area | 218 | Sycamore Street Rest Garden | 219 | Sycamore Street Sitting-out Area | 220 | Tai Kok Tsui Road/Larch Street Sitting-out Area | 221 | Temple Street/Kansu Street Temporary Rest Garden | 222 | Thistle Street Rest Garden | 223 | Tong Mei Road Sitting-out Area | 224 | Tong Mei Road/Tung Chau Street Sitting-out Area | 225 | Tung On Street Rest Garden | 226 | Waterloo Road/Canton Road Rest Garden | 227 | Waterloo Road/Wylie Road Sitting-out Area | 228 | Waterloo Road/Ferry Street Sitting-out Area | 229 | Wong Tai Street/Tai Tsun Street Sitting-out Area | 230 | Wong Tai Street/Ivy Street Sitting-out Area | 231 | Wylie Road Temporary Sitting-out Area | **232 | Yau Ma Tei Community Centre Rest Garden** | 233 | Yau Ma Tei Service Reservoir Rest Garden

Kowloon City

| 234 | Chatham Road/Winslow Street Sitting-out Area | 235 | Diocesan Boy's School Approach Road Sitting-out Area | 236 | Dorset Crescent Rest Garden | 237 | East Kowloon Way Flyover Rest Garden | **238 | Essex Crescent Rest Garden** | 239 | Fat Kwong Street Rest Garden | 240 | Ho Man Tin Hill Road Rest Garden | 241 | Hung Hom South Road Rest Garden | 242 | Hung Lai Road Sitting-out Area | 243 | Hung Ling Street Sitting-out Area | 244 | Kowloon City Road Flyover Sitting-out Area | 245 | Kwei Chow Street/Yut Yat Street Sitting-out Area | 246 | Lok Fu Service Reservoir Rest Garden | 247 | Lung Cheung Road Sitting-out Area | 248 | Ma Tau Wai Road/Tai Wan Road Sitting-out Area | 249 | Ma Tau Wai Road/Ma Hang Chung Road Rest Garden | 250 | Nga Tsin Wai Road Sitting-out Area | 251 | Pui Ching Road Rest Garden | 252 | Shek Ku Lung Road Rest Garden | 253 | Sheung Wo Street Sitting-out Area | 254 | Shing Tak Street Sitting-out Area | 255 | Station Lane Sitting-out Area | 256 | Sung On Street Sitting-out Area | 257 | Tak Ku Ling Road Rest Garden | 258 | Wa Shun Street Sitting-out Area | **259 | Yan Fung Street Rest Garden**

Wong Tai Sin

| 260 | Fei Fung Street Sitting-out Area | 261 | Hau Wong Temple Rest Garden | 262 | Heng Lam Street Sitting-out Area | 263 | Hong Keung Street Rest Garden | 264 | Junction Road/Fu Keung Street Sitting-out Area | **265 | Kam Fung Street Sitting-out Area** | 266 | King Fuk Street Sitting-out Area | 267 | Lok Sin Road/Choi Hung Road Sitting-out Area | 268 | Lung Cheung Road North/Po King Village Road Sitting-out Area | 269 | Nga Chin Wai Village Sitting-out Area | 270 | Ngau Chi Wan Street Temporary Sitting-out Area | 271 | Ngau Chi Wan Village Sitting-out Area | 272 | Po Kong Interchange Rest Garden | 273 | Po Kong Village Road/Shung Wah Street Sitting-out Area | 274 | Po Leung Lane Sitting-out Area | 275 | San Po Kong Interchange Rest Garden | 276 | San Po Kong Sitting-out Area | 277 | Shung Ling Street Sitting-out Area | 278 | Tsz Wan Shan Bus Terminus Sitting-out Area | 279 | Tsz Wan Shan Road Rest Garden | **280 | Tsz Wan Shan Road Sitting-out Area** | 281 | Wan Fung Street Sitting-out Area

Kwun Tong

| 282 | Cha Kwo Ling Village Sitting-out Area No.1 | 283 | Cha Kwo Ling Village Sitting-out Area No.2 | 284 | Choi Ha Road Sitting-out Area | 285 | Choi Wan Road Sitting-out Area | 286 | Clear Water Bay Road Temporary Sitting-out Area | 287 | Fan Wa Street Sitting-out Area | 288 | Fan Wa Street Temporary Sitting-out Area | 289 | Hiu Kwong Street Rest Garden | **290 | Hoi Bun Road Sitting-out Area** | 291 | Hong Lee Road Rest Garden | 292 | Hong Ning Road Rest Garden | 293 | Ka Wing Street Sitting-out Area | 294 | Kai Cheung Road Sitting-out Area | 295 | Kai Tin Road Sitting-out Area | 296 | Kai Yan Street Sitting-out Area | **297 | Ko Chiu Road Rest Garden** | 298 | Kwun Tong Road Rest Garden | 299 | Kwun Tong Road Sitting-out Area | 300 | Kwun Tong Road/Hip Wo Street Rest Garden | 301 | Lai Yip Street Sitting-out Area | 302 | Lam Fook Street Sitting-out Area | **303 | Lam Hing Street Sitting-out Area** | 304 | Lam Tin Bus Terminus Sitting-out Area | 305 | Lee On Road Sitting-out Area | **306 | Lei Yue Mun Rest Garden | 307 | Lei Yue Mun Typhoon Shelter Breakwater Sitting-out Area** | 308 | Lei Yue Mun Waterfront Sitting-out Area | **309 | Ma Yau Tong Central Sitting-out Area** | 310 | Ma Yau Tong West Sitting-out Area | 311 | New Clear Water Bay Road Sitting-out Area | 312 | Ngau Tau Kok Road Rest Garden | 313 | Pik Wan Road Rest Garden | 314 | Sau Ming Road Sitting-out Area | 315 | Sau Mau Ping Road/Hiu Kwong Street Sitting-out Area | 316 | Shing Yip Street Rest Garden | 317 | Shun On Road Sitting-out Area | 318 | Tai Yip Street Sitting-out Area | **319 | Ting Fu Street Sitting-out Area** | 320 | Ting Yu Square Temporary Sitting-out Area | **321 | Tsun Yip Cooked Food Market Roof-top Rest Garden** | 322 | Wai Yip Street Sitting-out Area | 323 | Wai Yip Street/Sheung Yee Road Sitting-out Area | 324 | Wan Hon Street Rest Garden | 325 | Wan Hon Street/Hip Wo Street Rest Garden | 326 | Wang Tai Road Sitting-out Area | 327 | Yau Tong Centre Rest Garden | 328 | Yee On Street Market Rest Garden | 329 | Yue Man Square Rest Garden

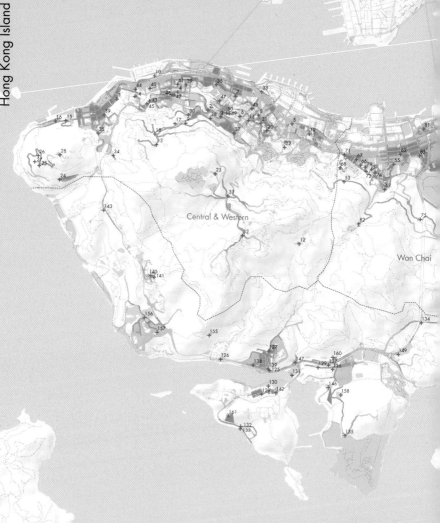

Hong Kong Island

Central & Western

Wan Chai

+   Sitting-out Area/Rest Garden

     Street and Walkway

     District Boundary

     Open Space

     5-min walk from SoA/RG

     10-min walk from SoA/RG

94
113   120   96 114
89
                                    100
                                 109   102 105
                                             118
                                          101
                                         111   107
                           124   110   108
                                       112 95 116
                                         97   103

Eastern
                                   92
                              106
                           113   93
                        104 122 123
                        97 150
                     92   99
                                         115

Southern

148

                                                        144 145

                      151
                   150
               152 153
                 139
                   154

                    0   0.5   1 KM   N

Sham Shui Po

Kowloon City

Yau Tsim Mong

+ Sitting-out Area/Rest Garden

Street and Walkway

District Boundary

Open Space

5-min walk from SoA/RG

10-min walk from SoA/RG

238

232

79

104

154

Lapse:
Heritage Signifier

Open space and collective memory. Framing, representing, incorporating and protecting; these Sitting-out Areas and Rest Gardens link to Hong Kong's corporeal histories, its forgotten artifacts and its intangible heritage – illuminating the layered city and its contradictions, overlapped readings and neighborhood stories.

238 Essex Crescent Rest Garden
Kowloon City
1,714 sqm

232 Yau Ma Tei Community
Centre Rest Garden
Yau Tsim Mong
2,080 sqm

79 Tai Wong Street East
Sitting-out Area
Wan Chai
369 sqm

104 Law Uk Folk Museum
Rest Garden
Eastern
6,391 sqm

154 Sun Pat Kan Sitting-out Area
Southern
272 sqm

Essex Crescent Rest Garden:
Bermuda Triangle

This small Rest Garden is located in Kowloon Tong, a historic garden city estate dating to the 1930s. The triangular garden is one of many green spaces within this planning area. Four large banyan trees, most likely planted when the park was built, dominate the site and are registered as "old and valuable trees" by the government. The surrounding walls and simple planting arrangements recall the original style, while the lack of maintenance implies a different sort of aging heritage.

Yau Ma Tei Community Centre Rest Garden:
Sacred Shelter

Fronting Tin Hau Temple and surrounded on three sides by lively market streets, this garden is a spacious resting place for local residents and a forecourt to the temple. The space is allocated with a repetition of simple elements: planter niches, benches and game tables. Occupants remain on site all day under the shade of a dense and mature banyan tree canopy – their bags and food containers revealing the subtle daily negotiations that claim and identify space.

Tai Wong Street East Sitting-out Area:
Reclamation Education

The physical form of this Sitting-out Area offers a visual representation of the land reclamation that took place in the late nineteenth century between Queens Road East and Johnston Road. The sequence of reclamations is actualized in miniature as a stepped platform, with the edge of each level cut in the shape of successive coastlines. Text embedded in the ground provides the historical facts related to each phase and refers to an information campaign of similarly themed displays throughout the area.

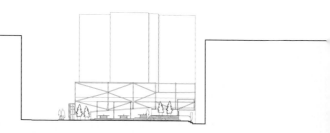

現有海岸線 EXISTING COASTLINE 2005

告士打道 GLOUCESTER ROAD 1964

RSITY ROAD 1924

Law Uk Folk Museum Rest Garden:
Ancestral Boundary

This Rest Garden constitutes the last evidence of Hakka Architecture in Chai Wan District. The site conserves both the cultural heritage of the Law Clan, and the landscape transformations that preceded the urbanization of Chai Wan. Once sited on the coastline, the garden is now surrounded by industrial and housing blocks. Sloping paths and shallow stairs preserve the general topography of the space but generic and ornamentally planted slopes hint at an underlying unease with the natural ecologies of the place.

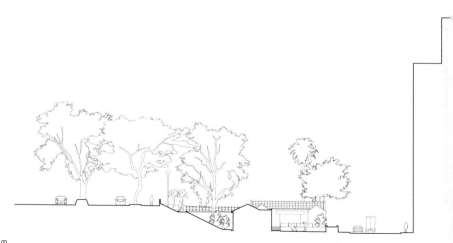

Sun Pat Kan Sitting-out Area:
At the Edge of History

This simple Sitting-out Area is located between Stanley Back Beach and the Pat Kan Uk heritage houses. Originally part of the front gardens of these dwellings, the site still holds four massive *Terminalia catappa* trees recognized as "old and valuable trees" by the government and honored by locals as *feng shui* trees in the settlement. This hard and soft heritage is acknowledged with a light intervention to protect the tree pit openings, surrounding them with custom-made wood benches.

196

280

319

44

32

115

143

147

161

Misfit:
Infrastructural Spanner

Between the city's smooth-flowing arterials and its pixelated edges, within the bulky networks of channel, culvert and reservoir as they intersect with rocky terrain, these Sitting-out Areas and Rest Gardens penetrate and occupy the three-dimensional city, mediating between the varied scales, speeds and territories of their supporting infrastructures.

Kowloon Park Drive Rest Garden:
Pocket with a Hole

This Rest Garden is located in a leftover wedge space between a ramping highway and the back of a row of commercial towers. Unlike many Rest Gardens, this space is only lightly planted in low ornamental arrangements. Though a short distance from Kowloon Park, the space is completely isolated from it. A market building that fills this same void sits at the back of it, providing a secondary entry to the site and stitching it to the surrounding urban area.

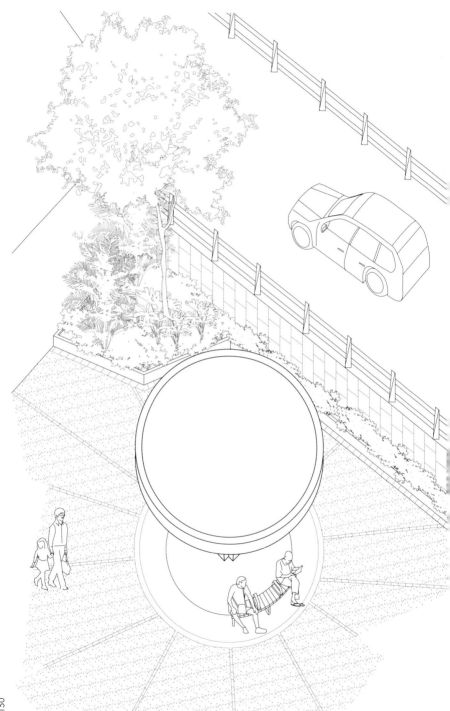

Tsz Wan Shan Road Sitting-out Area:
Shadowing Path

This long and narrow Sitting-out Area serves as a buffer between Tsz Wan Shan Road and the fresh-water reservoir below. The site features a single path that runs parallel with, but separate from, the adjacent sidewalk. The outer row of tall candlenut trees on one edge of this path double as the street trees. The space expands at the end of the 150 m path, resolving into a generous teardrop-shaped plaza with concentric seating and shading structures.

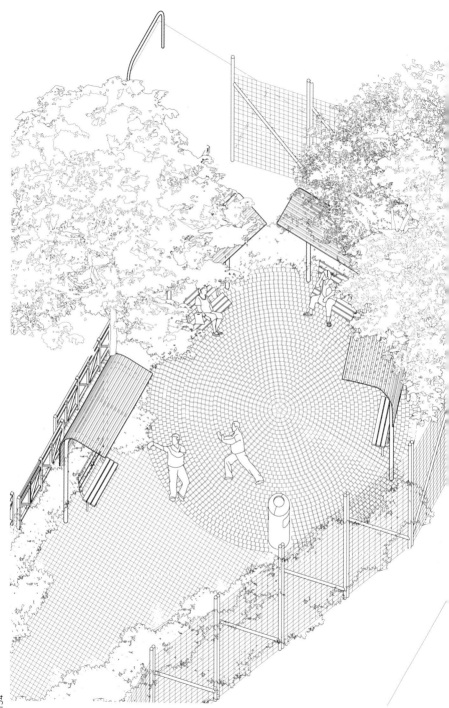

Ting Fu Street Sitting-out Area:
Buried Under the Flyover

This Sitting-out Area is located alongside Kwun Tong Road and below the raised dual trestles of the Kwun Tong MTR. Though there are four entrances, including a barrier free pathway, the site remains hidden behind the city's infrastructure. The linear space is buffered from its surroundings by densely vegetated planters supporting tall trees that seek light between the gaps in the structures above. Despite these softening efforts, noise from the adjacent roadway and trains above reverberates through the space.

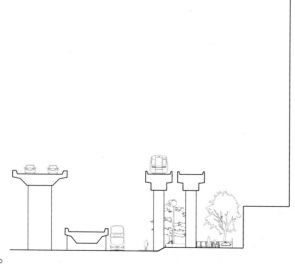

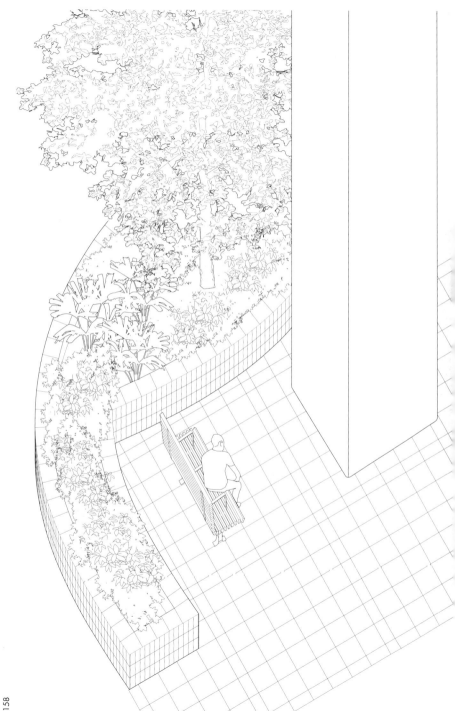

Sitting-out Area under the Flyover in Hill Road:
Besieged Bar

This Sitting-out Area occupies a site beneath an access-ramp flyover above Hill Road. Categorized as a temporary space and formed from the most basic pre-cast planters, seats and tables, the space is segregated from the adjacent pedestrian retail promenade. Only sparse vegetation survives here but hand-painted murals of historic motifs offer a relief from the concrete. Despite its poor quality, the site is usually full of residents from the nearby elderly centers.

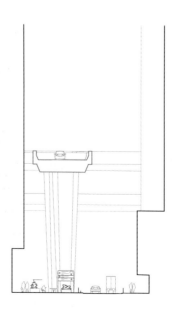

Peel Rise Rest Garden:
On the Slope

Located between Peak Road and Kellett Road in the Peak area, this
Rest Garden is a quiet space connecting two roads on different levels.
Trees and wildly vegetated retaining walls buffer the site from the
uphill road and mediate the slope, providing a single, triangular,
grassy yard. A traditional pavilion is the focal point of the space,
though a lone bench sits along the axial entry, facing-off with a
rubbish bin.

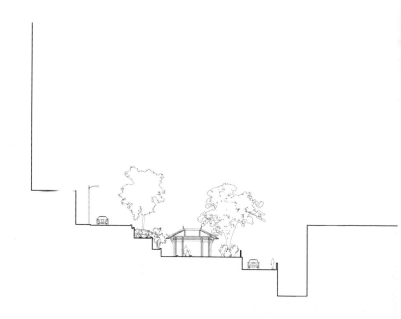

San Ha Street Sitting-out Area:
Sunbaked Slopes

This Sitting-out Area occupies a lobed-shaped site between three small streets that intersect on a slope. The site design is not particularly efficient and rather than mediating this slope, it provides a single square plaza set at the highest level. The lower half of the site is reduced to multiple, redundant stairs and tall, shotcrete-reinforced slopes. Though offering little seating, the Sitting-out Area provides a single, miniature plastic play-structure. With no shade and exposed to the west, however, the site seems to be put to better use to dry laundry.

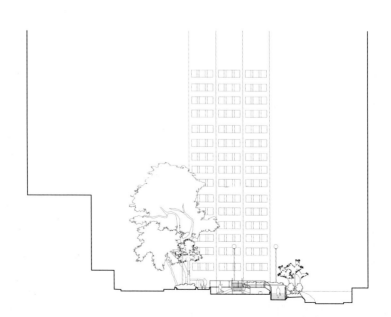

Sassoon Road Rest Garden:
Secret Underground

This small, ornately planted Rest Garden sits on a slope, and beneath an off-ramp flyover. It fills the circular void left from the interior turning radius and gradient of the looping roadway above it. The concrete highway structure above compresses the space to frame distant views of the city below. The site also serves as a path to link the nearby hospital, the bus stop and the upper and lower roads, allowing pedestrians to avoid the difficult road crossings on the highway level above.

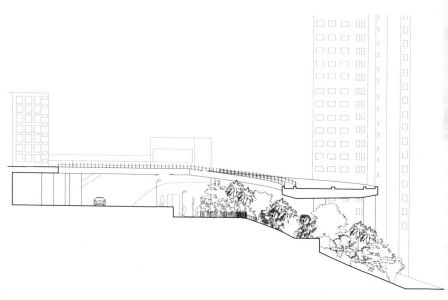

Sitting-out Area at Aberdeen Main Road/
Ap Lei Chau Bridge Flyover:
Trumpet Interchange

Occupying the circular ramp interchange between Ap Lei Chau
Bridge Road and Aberdeen Praya Road, this Sitting-out Area is a
transition between neighborhoods and levels. It shifts from an at-
grade road to the flyover space, from Wong Chuk Hang and Ap Lei
Chau; and from urban development to wild forested valley. Though
the site is dominated by a decorative response to the concentric road
geometry, a large portion of the useable area occupies the space
beneath the roadway.

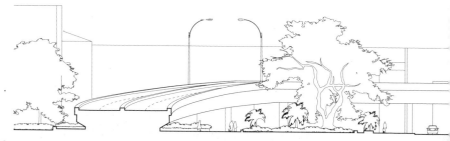

Yuk Kwai Shan Service Reservoir Sitting-out Area: Thin Roof Ranch

This Sitting-out Area is located on the lid structure of a large hillside reservoir. With the exception of a bare hill-cut on one corner, the site benefits from distant views of the harbor. The design of the space responds to this openness with a clutter of exercise equipment, prefab shelters, and randomly varied paving. In deference to structural constraints, there is no vegetation taller than grass grown in the space. Tall metal-mesh fencing encloses the space, somewhat pointlessly – a predictable reaction to codes unchallenged.

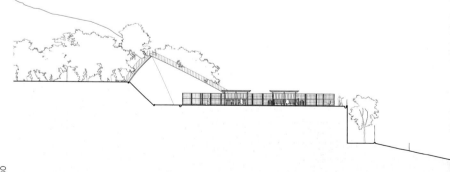

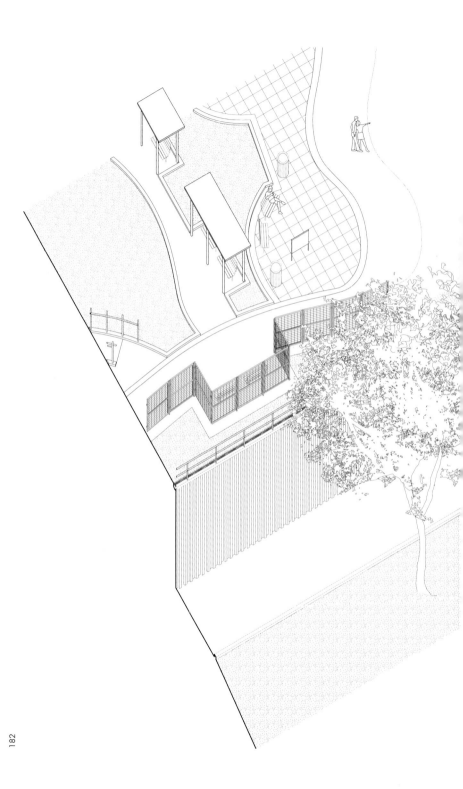

297

96

1

17

49

139

63

92

Rift:
Geodynamic Filler

Open space in an unstable terrain. Buttressed, retained, reinforced, cut-and-filled – the slopes of Hong Kong have been modified to maximize safety and developable area. Against these once unruly surfaces and in the cracks and ledges that aren't otherwise commodified, the Sitting-out Area finds its precarious purchase.

297 Ko Chiu Road Rest Garden
     Kwun Tong
     1,362 sqm

96   Comfort Terrace Rest Garden
     Eastern
     718 sqm

1   Belcher's Street
     Sitting-out Area
     Central & Western
     200 sqm

17   Kotewall Road Rest Garden
     Central & Western
     348 sqm

49   Wing Lee Street Rest Garden
     Central & Western
     1,560 sqm

139 Old Main Street Rest Garden
     Southern
     251 sqm

63   Kennedy Street
     Sitting-out Area
     Wan Chai
     233 sqm

92   Chai Wan Road Temporary
     Rest Garden
     Eastern
     94 sqm

Ko Chiu Road Rest Garden:
Hide and Seek

This Rest Garden, built in the 1970s during a surge of housing construction, was designed to provide a passive amenity space for nearby residents. Generous paths, terraces and pavilions are complemented by mature planting. However, following a recent redevelopment of the area, the Rest Garden today is largely hidden in the densely vegetated slope. Once a local destination, the site is now utilized as a cross-slope shortcut between the shopping mall below it and the public estates above.

Comfort Terrace Rest Garden:
Shaft Landscape

Located within a residential area on the narrow, reinforced slope
this Sitting-out Area is situated between a single-lane road below
and the entrance to a residential tower above. The remnant space
is dominated by a sculptural ventilation shaft piercing the concrete
ground from the MTR station tunneling below. This tower is a threshold
at the site entry with a small plaza and an awkwardly juxtaposed
pavilion beyond. An upper retaining wall supports two large *Ficus
microcarpa* trees.

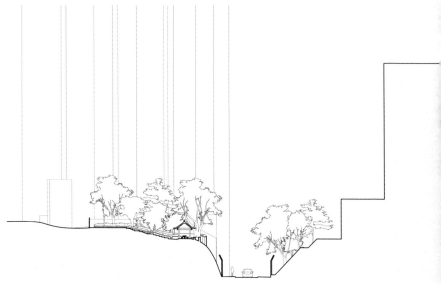

Belcher's Street Sitting-out Area:
Urban Fortress in the Gap

This Sitting-out Area is built within a concrete-reinforced slope tha
reaches down steeply to a narrow sidewalk in Kennedy Town. Cu
into the shallow space available to it, the site design negotiates the
rocky slope face, utility structures and drainage pipes with a small
trellis-covered seating area and utilitarian stairs and guardrails. A big
banyan tree, which in all likelihood predates the construction of this
space, grips the underlying rock face and shades the seating areas.

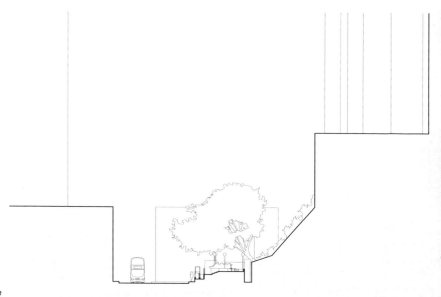

Kotewall Road Rest Garden:
Healing and Memory

This Rest Garden occupies the site of the former Kotewall Cour residential building, which was destroyed by a large landslide or June 18, 1972. The public space forms part of the slope reinforcemen work undertaken after the landslide and doubles as a memorial. Waterfalls and staggered stairs mediate the elevation change from Kotewall Road to the sitting areas below. Water, intended as c soothing feature in the space is a reminder of the liquid terrains o Hong Kong.

Wing Lee Street Rest Garden:
Wave Garden

This shotcrete-formed space is located on a slope between two "stair
streets in a predominantly residential area. The garden is secluded
and difficult to stumble on for anyone other than the residents of the
area. A path, oriented parallel to the slope, splits along its length
to define upper and lower seating platforms. Despite the ubiquitous
shotcrete ground, the space feels cool and green with mature tree
sprouting from small holes in the slope to form a complete canopy.

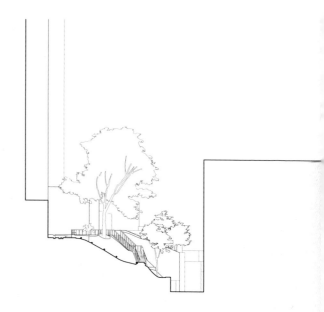

Old Main Street Rest Garden:
Corner of Consciousness

This small Rest Garden occupies a triangular slope fragment between an alleyway of traditional temples and the flat boundary road of Aberdeen's town center. The site is terraced into the slope as two levels, with entrances at upper and lower levels forming a cross-slope shortcut to the settlement areas above. Long benches and the custom pavilion architecture, alongside the elements of cultural heritage, give the space a unique feeling and offer an ideal gathering space for groups exploring the area.

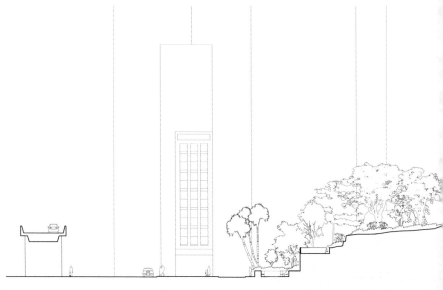

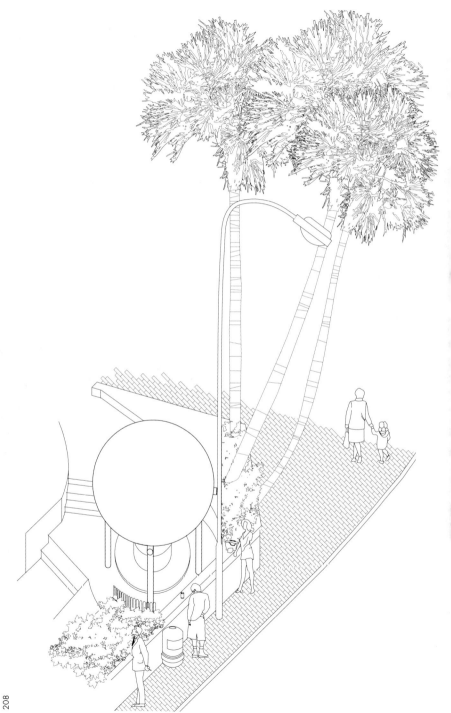

Kennedy Street Sitting-out Area:
Wall Park

This Sitting-out Area is built into the stepped retaining walls that separate two socially and topographically distinct neighborhoods – the Mid-levels and Wan Chai. Stairs, ramping paths and small terraces fill the odd void between the faceted walls, concrete-covered slopes and a traditional temple. Oriented north, well-vegetated and situated below the surrounding development, this moss-covered site is in near perpetual shade and hosts a microclimate distinct from its urban surroundings.

Chai Wan Road Temporary Rest Garden:
The Stair Wags the Garden

This tiny space is among the smallest Sitting-Out Areas or Rest Gardens in Hong Kong. Sitting at the bottom of a remnant slope between two development sites, it accommodates a rectangular platform, and is surrounded by tall planters that buffer the space against the heavy traffic on Chai Wan Road. The Rest Garden benefits from the spatial release of the vegetated terrain behind it, through which an intimate stairway weaves its way upwards to Tai Tam Road.

290

307

306

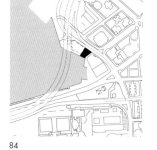

84

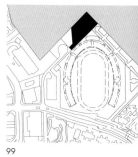

99

Littoral:
Terrestrial Anchor

Open space at the watery edge, the shifting edge, the artificial edge. Layering, projecting, protecting in sand, stone, concrete, and wood. These Sitting-out Areas and Rest Gardens are links to a new public-realm network focused on the amenity of Hong Kong's Victoria Harbour – linking emerging forms of active recreation with traditional and passive practices of occupying the harbor front.

290 Hoi Bun Road
Sitting-out Area
Kwun Tong
893 sqm

307 Lei Yue Mun Typhoon Shelter
Breakwater Sitting-out Area
Kwun Tong
1331 sqm

306 Lei Yue Mun Rest Garden
Kwun Tong
1989 sqm

84 Whitfield Road Rest Garden
Wan Chai
498 sqm

99 Fu Hong Street
Sitting-out Area
Eastern District
4212 sqm

Hoi Bun Road Sitting-out Area:
Plaster Promenade

This newly built Sitting-Out Area is part of an area-wide urban regeneration program and forms a narrow public space that extends along the waterfront access from the larger Kwun Tong promenade and ferry pier. One edge anchors an awkward gap between the sidewalk and sea wall, and includes benches and two sculptural pavilions. The space sports a mix of characters: sleek glass guardrails provide visual access to the water, while wooden "boardwalks" suggest a beachfront rustic.

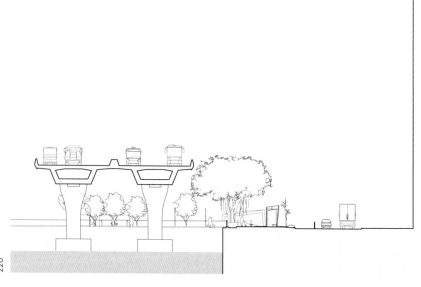

Lei Yue Mun Typhoon Shelter Breakwater Sitting-out Area
Grounded Raft

Typhoon Shelters are remnants of the once widespread water-born settlements of Hong Kong. This Sitting-out Area is an active, lined space occupying the shelter's breakwater jetty. The design draws o cultural imagery, with fish-themed planters and traditional pavilions The site is activated by crisscrossing ramps and open edges for fishin and boat access. An open center allows larger social gatherings an also functions as a waiting area for the nearby ferry.

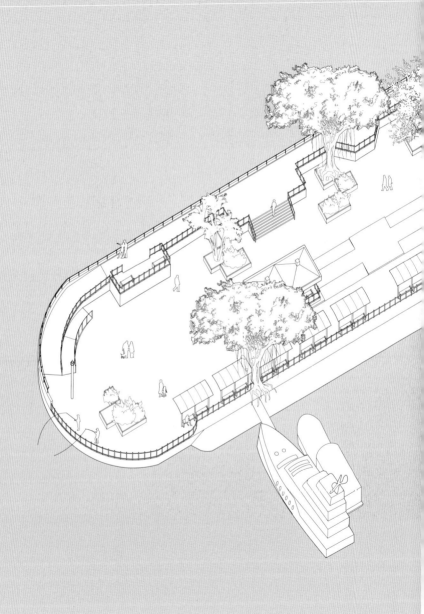

Lei Yue Mun Rest Garden:
Deep Perspective

A waterfront adjacent to an old coastal village, this Rest Garden is a community space, designed to serve local residents and workers. Platforms and walkways are oriented towards the picturesque views of Victoria Harbour. Massive planters divide the site into smaller rooms with plentiful perimeter seating and covered pavilions. Against this interiority, a single platform reaches out towards the harbor, capturing a rare sandy shoreline.

Whitfield Road Rest Garden:
Tranquil Fringe

Set amongst a tangle of flyovers and tunnels, a utility substation and a fire station, this Rest Garden is sited at a nearly invisible, inaccessible corner of the Causeway Bay Typhoon Shelter. In contrast to the modern office buildings and upgraded infrastructure that surround it, the space is designed to suggest a traditional garden. But the Chinese pavilion screens a machine room, and the Gongshi rock arrangements are actually painted concrete. These elements reveal the artificiality of the site and the constructed ground on which it sits.

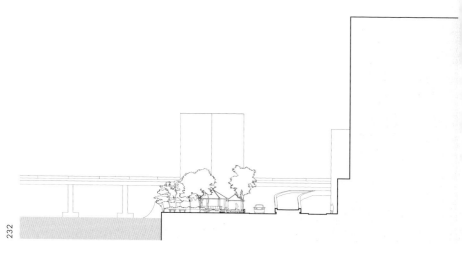

Fu Hong Street Sitting-out Area:
Seats and Circuits

This large Sitting-out Area lies adjacent to a series of local open spaces that together form a nearly continuous cycling and jogging path, which in turn connects to a regional park and trail system in the Siu Sai Wan area. The space is well used for recreation by children and families. Despite its dramatic harbor-front views, the site pulls away from the sea wall and instead is organized around two generic pavilions located in the middle of the space.

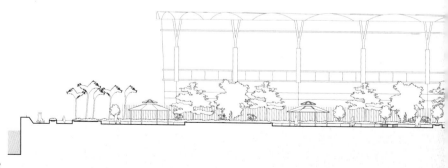

265

303

205

51

321

35

40

48

Gap:
Density Deconstructor

Density's foil. Interior's relief. Filling setbacks, expanding alleys, occupying lots. These Sitting-out Areas and Rest Gardens follow the uneven metabolism of the city's regeneration as they cluster in areas of transformation – filling the interstitial fragments between developments, or cut from the warp and weft of the city's dense urban fabric.

265 Kam Fung Street
Sitting-out Area
Wong Tai Sin
492 sqm

303 Lam Hing Street
Sitting-out Area
Kwun Tong
884 sqm

205 Portland Street Rest Garden
Yau Tsim Mong
377 sqm

51 Amoy Street Sitting-out Area
Wan Chai
348 sqm

321 Tsun Yip Cooked Food
Market Roof-top Rest Garden
Kwun Tong
1,483 sqm

35 Pokfield Road
Sitting-out Area
Central & Western
125 sqm

40 Sai On Lane Rest Garden
Central & Western
885 sqm

48 Wa On Lane Sitting-out Area
Central & Western
270 sqm

Kam Fung Street Sitting-out Area:
Where the Phoenix Rests

Located in Wong Tai Sin, the district in Hong Kong with the largest population of elderly people, this Sitting-out Area is an active social gathering place. It is situated in a residential estate, between a bus stop and an amenity shopping area. With abundant shade and covered seating, this strip of open space serves as a public living room for its nearby residents.

Lam Hing Street Sitting-out Area:
Industrial Green

Located in the industrial core of Kowloon Bay, this Sitting-out Area, together with four others like it, form a series of green passageways. They provide infiltration and pedestrian circulation between the surrounding built-up blocks. Proportioned as a roadway, the green link is in fact defined by a single hardscape path between continuous planters. These screen the adjacent buildings and offer a tree-canopied corridor for its users. The consistent form and material choices in each Sitting-out Area unifies them into a single urban gesture.

Portland Street Rest Garden:
Space Geometry

This small Rest Garden is located in an empty lot in the busy Yau Ma
Tei area and functions as a gathering space for resting tourists and
residents. The space within the site is delineated by low, honeycomb
shaped planters of small palms and generic shrubs, and clusters of
covered seating. The width of the site faces the street, and the planters
and signage placed to seclude it provide little sense of enclosure
against the clearly defined edges of the adjacent residential blocks.

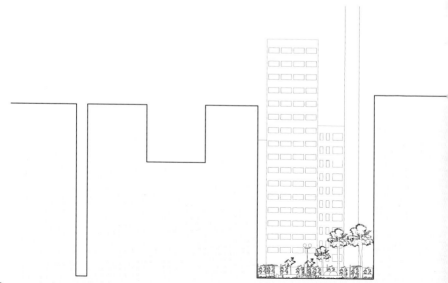

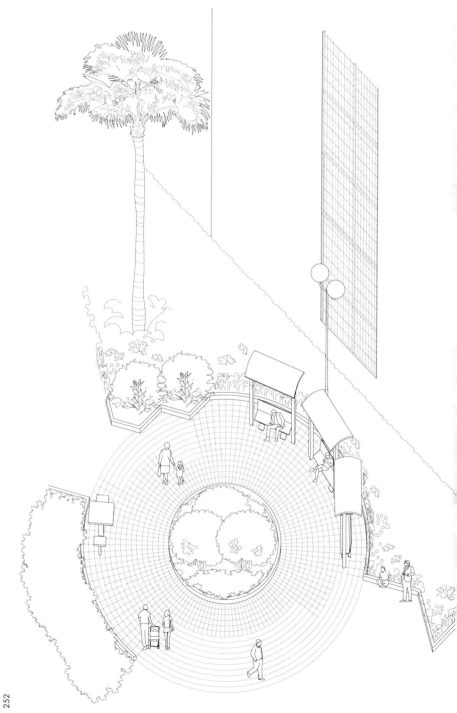

Amoy Street Sitting-out Area:
Back to Baroque

This newly built Sitting-out Area is part of the controversial urban renewal project around Lee Tung Street. Its classically detailed terraces, steps and planters are congruent with the faux-European style of the new development block. The Sitting-out Area provides a generously planted public realm asset and cross-link within the privately managed enclave space at the development's core. A pedestrian bridge linking the residential podium above, serves as a reminder of the site's true occupants.

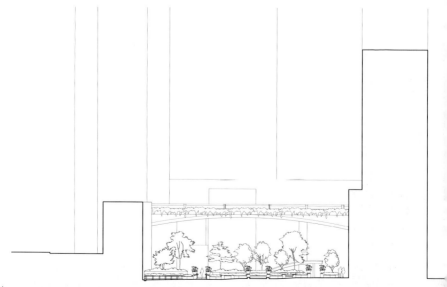

Tsun Yip Cooked Food Market Roof-Top Rest Garden: Elevated Oasis

This Rest Garden occupies the entire roof of a "cooked-food" municipal market building. The low-slung but elevated site is surrounded by the tall new commercial towers and industrial-office buildings found in the developing core of Kwun Tong. The design of the site features numerous heavy shelters and plaster-white sculptural planters that camouflage the bulky exhaust units on the roof. The site, removed from the street as it is, is rarely visited and poorly maintained.

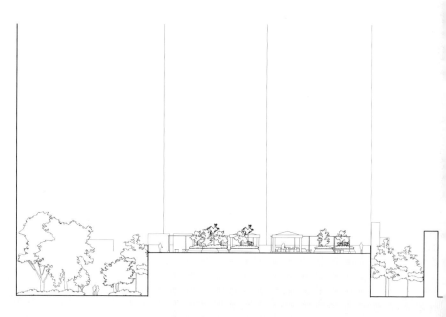

Pokfield Road Sitting-out Area:
Continuous Wrapper

This Sitting-out Area is elevated from the street level, its two open edges formed by a tall, mural-covered retaining wall. Despite its location in a residential area, the site is invisible from the street itself and its occupants are shielded from public scrutiny. On the inside, planters with long, integral benches break up the space into two cells, though the soil areas within them remain too thin to hold more than a line of skinny palm trees.

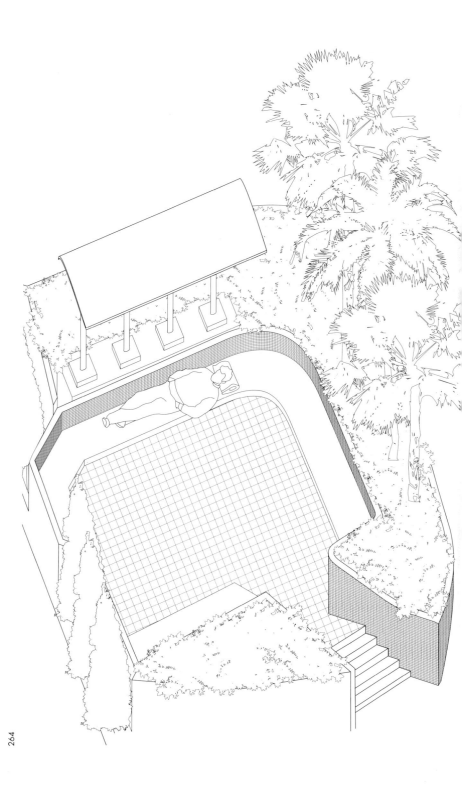

Sai On Lane Rest Garden:
Stinky Oasis

Located in an alleyway between two major arterials in Sai Wan, this Rest Garden is surrounded by tall residential buildings. The space is not easily accessible and is poorly ventilated and dark. Kitchen exhaust flavors the greasy air. Surprisingly, the site itself has been carefully designed as a series of interlocking spaces that are separated by angled planters with integral seating. Tiled walls, floors and structures add a vintage texture to the space, while shade-loving vegetation thinly screens the surrounding buildings.

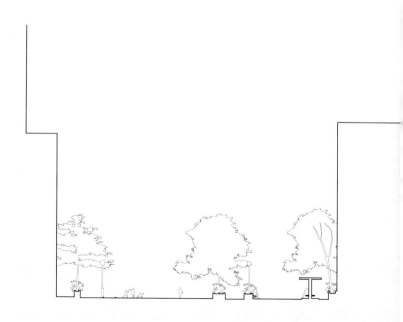

Wa On Lane Sitting-out Area:
A Landscape Secreted Away

Hidden behind dense retail frontage and residential buildings, this Sitting-out Area ties together the back-areas and alleys within the block, along a sloping topography. The space is stacked in three levels, each with a corresponding entry gateway that is simultaneously inviting and invisible to an unknowing public. The terraces create a dynamic experience, and movement between them is celebrated in sculptural staircases and ramps that lend a maze-like sense to the circulation.

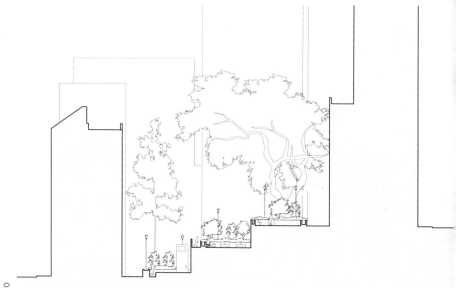

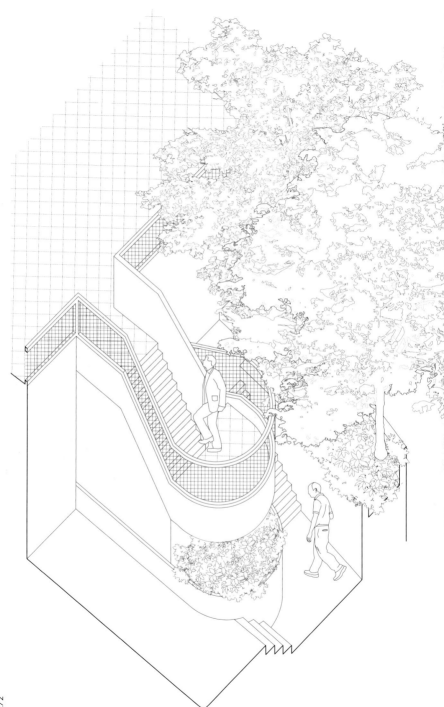

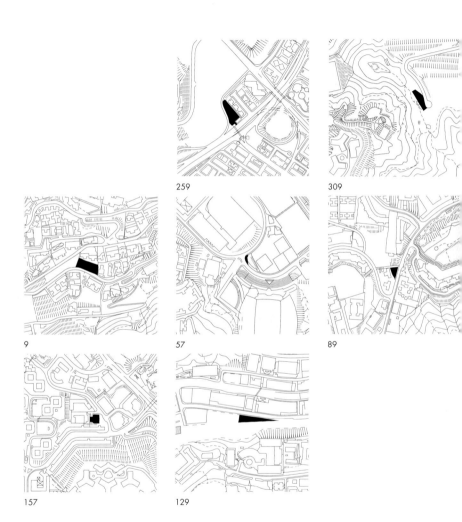

259

309

9

57

89

157

129

Lacuna:
Ecological Amplifier

Fragmented, altered and artificially sustained by design, or by dereliction, these Sitting-out Areas and Rest Gardens borrow the surrounding landscapes and urban forest in an extension of their own miniature environments. Sculpting space with vegetation, these sites shift local microclimates and alter the flows of water, wind and organisms throughout the city.

259 Yan Fung Street Rest Garden
     Kowloon City
     1,733 sqm

309 Ma Yau Tong Central
     Sitting-out Area
     Kwun Tong
     1,116 sqm

9   Conduit Road Rest Garden
     Central & Western
     1,957 sqm

57   Eastern Hospital Road
     Sitting-out Area
     Wan Chai
     425 sqm

89   Breamer Hill Road
     Sitting-out Area
     Eastern
     468 sqm

157 Wah Lam Path
     Sitting-out Area
     Southern
     692 sqm

129 Heung Yip Road SoA
     Southern
     1356 sqm

Yan Fung Street Rest Garden:
City Lungs

This Rest Garden is located at the junction of a busy road and a quiet street, providing a separate pedestrian connection between the upper and lower areas it sits between and a brief relief from nearby traffic. Mature trees on the site indicate that the ground of the space has been an urban green for many years. Raised above the surrounding levels, the space is a green island in dense urban surroundings, creating a link between the wooded valleys of the nearby hills and the urban forest in the city area.

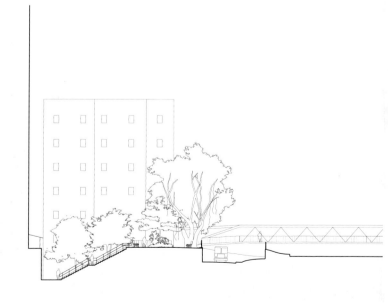

Ma Yau Tong Central Sitting-out Area:
Fabricated Plateau

This Sitting-out Area is located at the ridge of a large public park in the slopes above Lam Tin. It occupies a former landfill and presents itself as an incongruously flat and treeless void in the surrounding forested terrain – a hint at the unnatural, untenable soils below. The space is mostly paved and fully fenced but the small green areas and tall conical planters in the site are slowly re-wilding – a consequence of poor maintenance and an abundance of nearby seed stock.

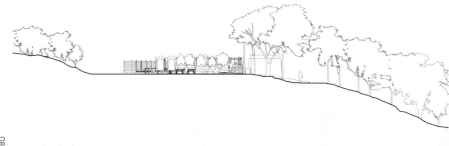

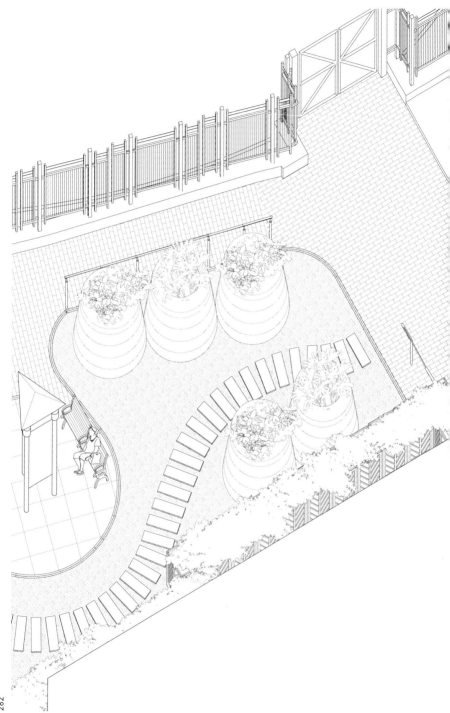

Conduit Road Rest Garden:
Forest Path

This Rest Garden occupies a steeply sloped site and is accessed from a single stairway that opens directly on to a busy roadway. The 1,900-sqm site backs onto Victoria Peak and is surrounded by remnant woodlands and luxury residential towers. A narrow path lined with a few seats completes a ramping, stepped loop within the boundary of the site. Though lacking in program, the space is planted with an exuberant mix of ferns, palms, palmettos and ficus that links it with the surrounding hybrid ecologies.

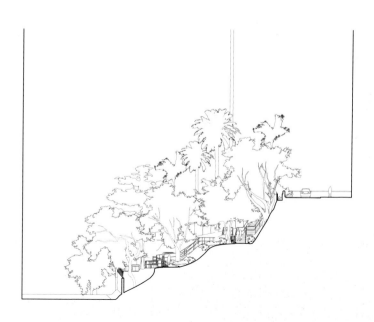

Eastern Hospital Road Sitting-out Area:
A Corner with a Sense of Form

This Sitting-out Area occupies a leftover sliver of space between Eastern Hospital, Caroline Hill Road and the rectangular pitches of the Indian Recreation Club, on the lower slopes of Happy Valley's forested ridge. The space is abundantly vegetated for a Sitting-out Area, with narrow planters and large pot containers defining the seating and the circulation zones.

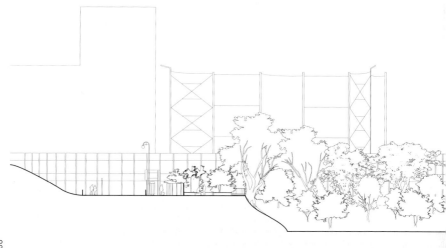

Breamer Hill Rd Sitting-out Area:
Marginal Green

More than 90% of this Sitting-out Area is inaccessible. The vegetated interior is completely enclosed behind a conspicuous and continuous steel mesh fence wall. At the perimeter, sheltered benches face outwards along the street and the nearby bus stop but away from the green areas behind. Undisturbed and largely unmaintained, grasses and clumps of shrubs such as magnolia, pine, sabina, cypress, schefflera and berberis thrive in this miniature artificial ecology – forming an emerging wilderness in the city.

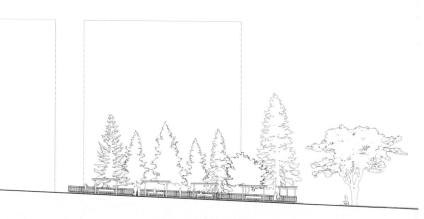

Wah Lam Path Siting-out Area:
Foundation Garden

This Sitting-out Area lies adjacent to a large public housing estate and various institutional buildings. Located on a slope and not easily accessed, the site is poorly used despite the dense settlement surrounding it. Custom details, materials, a classic layout and the abundant vegetation give the space an exclusive atmosphere. Though green, the plants constitute a banal, artificial ecology with the most common trees of Hong Kong, *Ficus microcarpa*, *Michelia alba* and *Bauhinia blakeana*, utilized throughout.

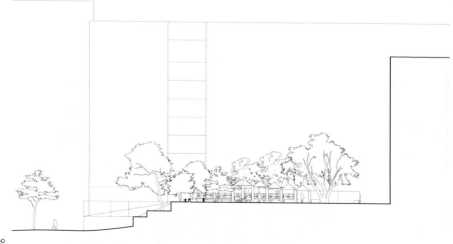

Heung Yip Rd Sitting-out Area:
Canal-Front Deviations

This Sitting-out Area fills a wedge of land between the channel of what was once Staunton Creek, and Heung Yip Road. Formerly an industrial area, the streetscape and canal are now an important link to the Wong Chuk Hang MTR. The space is organized as a single bed of dense planting that extends to the site's boundaries. Against this green background, a broad path and a vine-planted trellis carve a zigzagging route that compresses and extends the space along the canal.

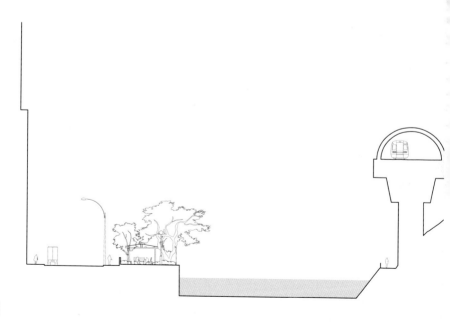

During the course of the research, three public exhibitions were held in Shanghai, Hong Kong and Guangzhou to engage the public on the topic of small-scale public space.

Interstitial Hong Kong Exhibition, Shanghai
October 28, 2017–January 6, 2018
Public Gallery, HKU Shanghai Study Center

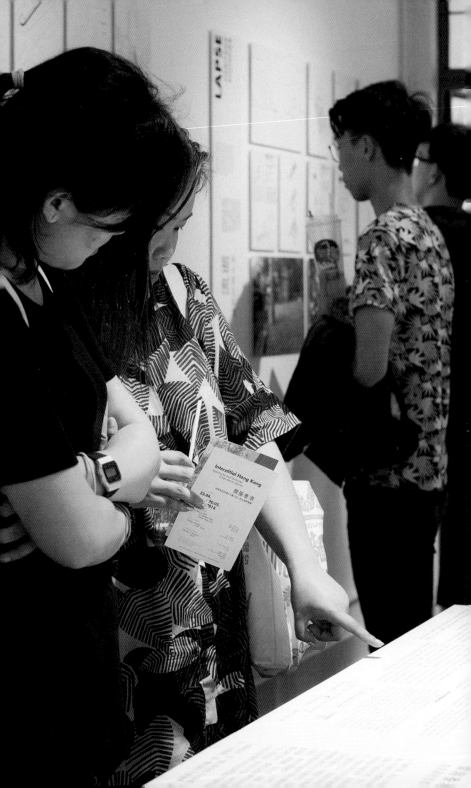

Interstitial Hong Kong Exhibition, Hong Kong
April 22–May 20, 2018
PMQ

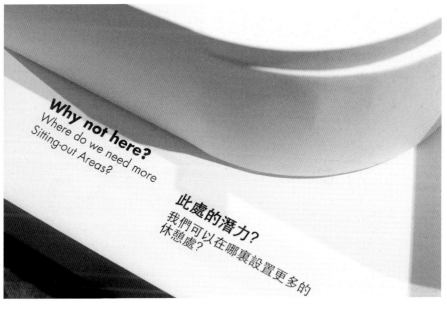

Interstitial Hong Kong Exhibition, Hong Kong
April 22–May 20, 2018
PMQ

Interstitial Hong Kong Exhibition, Guangzhou
July 21–August 31, 2018
The Borderless Wall, Fei Arts Museum

Authors

Alain Chiaradia is an architect, urban designer and Associate Professor at the Department of Planning and Design at the University of Hong Kong, where he also directs the Master of Urban Design program. Alain is interested in bridging macro to micro scales of urban design and research. He led the conceptual development of 3D spatial design network analysis software (sDNA) and develops urban morphometrics to capture the impacts and values of urban design.

Melissa Cate Christ is a Research Assistant Professor at Hong Kong Polytechnic University, a registered landscape architect (Canada) and the founding director of transverse studio. Previously she taught at the University of Hong Kong and the University of Toronto and worked at Gustafson Guthrie Nichol (GGN) and du Toit Allsopp Hillier (DTAH). She has a Master of Landscape Architecture from the University of Toronto and a Bachelor of Liberal Arts from St. John's College.

Xiaoxuan Lu is an Assistant Professor in the Division of Landscape Architecture at the University of Hong Kong, where she teaches landscape history and theory, and design studios. Her research focuses on the cultural landscape and geography of conflict, particularly in transboundary regions. She received her Bachelor of Architecture from Southern California Institute of Architecture, Master in Landscape Architecture from Harvard University and PhD in Human Geography from Peking University.

Andrew Toland is a Lecturer in Landscape Architecture at the University of Technology Sydney. Prior to that he taught at the University of Hong Kong. He holds degrees in architecture, law and economics. His research examines the cultural and social dimensions of large-scale landscape infrastructures and technologies, the conceptualization of the nonhuman in design and landscape practices and discourses of realism and post-reality in architecture, landscape architecture and urbanism.

Susanne Trumpf is a Senior Lecturer in the Division of Landscape Architecture at the University of Hong Kong, where she teaches design studios and landscape media. She has previously taught at Hong Kong Polytechnic University, the AA Visiting School (Hong Kong), and Hong Kong Design Institute. Susanne has practiced in Berlin and Hong Kong and is founder of indialogue. She graduated from TU Berlin, Germany (BArch), and from TU Delft, Netherlands (MArch), in Architecture, Urbanism and Building Sciences.

Ivan Valin is an Assistant Professor of Landscape Architecture in the Division of Landscape Architecture at the University of Hong Kong, where he also directed the Masters and Post-graduate Diploma programs. His research examines the planned and accidental landscape systems in the tropics, especially in the context of rapid urbanization. Ivan is a founding partner of valeche studio and holds a Master of Architecture and Master of Landscape Architecture from the University of California, Berkeley.

Lingzhu Zhang is a Post-doctoral Fellow at the Department of Urban Planning and Design, the University of Hong Kong where she lectures on urban design technologies and innovations. Her research combines network science and un/supervised machine learning techniques, examining urban design and public realm design impacts on livability and vitality. She is a registered architect in China and holds a joint PhD from Tongji University and Cardiff University.

Acknowledgments

Initial research for this project was supported by the Division of Landscape Architecture at the University of Hong Kong, and the related exhibitions were funded in part by Design Trust, a Hong Kong–based grant funding platform. Funding for this book was provided by the Design Publication Fund from the Department of Architecture at the University of Hong Kong.

We thank the Master of Landscape Architecture student cohorts of 2016, 2017 and 2018 for the enthusiasm and insight that they brought to the teaching component of this research project and in particular to the case study documentation at its core. We would especially like to recognize Hok Ming Chan, Xubin Chen, Yuk Lun Chong, Yik Ming Tsang and Oi Ling Wong for their contributions to the illustrations and photographs that appear in this volume. We are also grateful to Vincci Mak and Jason Hilgefort for their engagement with the work as co-instructors in the MLA studio with us in 2017 and 2018. Finally, we are grateful to Gavin Coates, Anita Dawood and Colin Sutcliffe, who provided exceptional editorial input and polish for the English texts.

The following students are responsible for the initial case study survey and analysis work that is featured in the second part of the book: Chung Yan Au Young, Wenwen Cai, Daniel Francisco Cevallos, Howe Chan, Ka Ying Chan, Ka Yu Chan, Wing Ka Cheung, Shing Chun Chu, Junyi Fan, Jialei He, Ka Ho Ip, Yat Fung Kwong, So Man Lai, Pung Chin Li, Ricki Lip, Wing Yin Luk, Naijin Pan, Zongyi Qian, Kanisa Sattayanurak, Siu Kei Shum, Ruoxi Tian, Xuting Wang, Hoo Ming Wong, Hiu Yan Wong, Wing Yin Wong, Chi Wai Wu, Tsz Ching Yan, Chun Ting Yau, Boyang Zhang, Shaoyin Zhang, Wenli Zhang, Yuwei Zhao, Danying Zheng, Ying Zheng and Yifan Zhou.

Cover: Xubin Chen

Design and setting: Xiaoxuan Lu, Susanne Trumpf and Ivan Valin
Lithography: Bild1Druck, Berlin
Printed in the European Union.

Bibliographic information published by the Deutsche
Nationalbibliothek.
The Deutsche Nationalbibliothek lists this publication in the
Deutsche Nationalbibliografie. Detailed bibliographic data are
available on the Internet at http://dnb.d-nb.de.

jovis Verlag GmbH
Lützowstraße 33
10785 Berlin

www.jovis.de

jovis books are available worldwide in select bookstores.
Please contact your nearest bookseller or visit www.jovis.de for
information concerning your local distribution.

ISBN 978-3-86859-689-2 (Flexcover)
ISBN 978-3-86859-959-6 (PDF)